MACMILLAN
MUSIC and YOU

MACMILLAN
MUSIC and YOU

Barbara Staton, Senior Author
Merrill Staton, Senior Author
Marilyn Davidson
Phyllis Kaplan

Susan Snyder, contributing author

Macmillan Publishing Company

New York

ACKNOWLEDGMENTS

Grateful acknowledgment is given to the following authors and publishers. In the case of some songs and poems for which acknowledgment is not given, we have earnestly endeavored to find the original source and to procure permission for their use, but without success. Extensive research failed to locate the author and/or copyright holder.

Alfred Publishing Company for *Clickety Clack* by Martha and Hap Palmer from HAP PALMER FAVORITES, 1981. Used by Permission of the Publisher.

Belwin-Mills for *Little Spotted Puppy* and *I Made a Valentine* from SONGS FOR OUR SMALL WORLD by Lynn Freeman Olson and Georgia Garlid. Copyright © 1968 by Schmitt Music Center, a division of Belwin-Mills Publishing Corp. Used by permission. All rights reserved. For *Hear the Bells Ring* from SAFARI by Konnie Saliba. Copyright © 1976 by Belwin-Mills Publishing Corp. Used by permission. All rights reserved.

Birch Tree Group for *A La Puerta del Cielo*, adapted by Augustus D. Zanzig. From *Birchard Music Series, Book 5*. Copyright 1962 Birch Tree Group Ltd. All rights reserved. Used by permission. For *I've a Pair of Fishes*, words by J. Lilian Vandevere. From Birchard Music Series Book 2. Copyright © 1962 by Birch Tree Group Ltd. Used by permission. All rights reserved.

Board of Jewish Education for *Little Candle Fires* from SONGS FOR CHILDREN by Hyman Reznick, composers S.E. Goldfarb and S.S. Grossman. Reprinted courtesy of the Board of Jewish Education.

Milton Bradley Co. for the words to *When You Send a Valentine* by Mildred J. Hill from Emilie Poulsson's HOLIDAY SONGS.

Brandt & Brandt for *Abraham Lincoln* by Rosemary Carr and Stephen Vincent Benet. From A BOOK OF AMERICANS by Rosemary and Stephen Vincent Benet. Copyright 1933 by Rosemary and Stephen Vincent Benet. Copyright renewed © 1961 by Rosemary Carr Benet. Reprinted by permission of Brandt & Brandt Literary Agents, Inc.

Chappell & Co. Inc. for the words to *Frosty the Snowman* by Steve Nelson & Jack Rollins. Copyright © 1950 by Hill & Range Songs, Inc. Copyright renewed, assigned to Chappell & Co., Inc. (Intersong Music, Publisher). International Copyright Secured. ALL RIGHTS RESERVED. Used by permission. For *Peter Cottontail* by Steve Nelson & Jack Rollins. Copyright © 1950 by Hill & Range Songs, Inc. Copyright renewed, assigned to Chappell & Co., Inc. (Intersong Music, Publisher). International Copyright Secured. ALL RIGHTS RESERVED. Used by permission.

Nancy Dervan for *A Time for Love* from PIECES AND PROCESS NO. 4 "CHRISTMAS TIDINGS," 1980. Copyright © 1985 by Nancy Dervan. Reprinted by permission.

E.P. Dutton for *Furry Bear* from NOW WE ARE SIX by A.A. Milne. Copyright 1927 by E.P. Dutton, renewed 1955 by A.A. Milne. Reprinted by permission of the publisher, E.P. Dutton, a division of New American Library. For *Happiness* from WHEN WE WERE VERY YOUNG by A.A. Milne. Copyright 1924 by E.P. Dutton, renewed 1952 by A.A. Milne. Reprinted by permission of the publisher, E.P. Dutton, a division of New American Library.

Theresa Fulbright for *Martin Luther King* from THE SPECTRUM OF MUSIC, Grade 2, by Marsh, Rinehart, and Savage. Copyright © 1974 Macmillan Publishing Co., Inc. Reprinted by permission.

Ginn & Co. for the music to *When You Send a Valentine* by Louella Garrett from "SINGING ON OUR WAY" of OUR SINGING WORLD series. Copyright © 1959, 1957, 1949, by Ginn and Co. Used by permission.

Harper & Row for *Autumn Woods* from CRICKETY CRICKETY: The Best Loved Poems of James S. Tippett. Copyright 1933 by Harper & Row Publishers, Inc. Renewed 1961 by Martha K. Tippett. Reprinted by permission of Harper & Row, Publishers, Inc. For *Come Skating* from A LIGHT IN THE ATTIC. Poems and drawings by Shel Silverstein. Copyright © 1981 by Snake Eye Music, Inc. Reprinted by permission of Harper & Row, Publishers, Inc. For *Our Flag* (first line "There Are Many Flags in Many Lands") by Mary Howliston from THE GOLDEN FLUTE, selected by Alice Hubbard and Adeline Babbitt (John Day Co.). Copyright 1932, 1960 by Harper & Row, Publishers, Inc. Reprinted by permission of Harper & Row, Publishers, Inc.

W.S. Haynie for *Shake the Papaya Down* collected by W.S. Haynie. Copyright 1966, Gulf Music Co. Used by permission.

D.C. Heath for *False Face* by David Russell and Susan Rupert from MUSIC FOR YOUNG AMERICANS by Richard Berg, Claudene Burns, Daniel Hooley, Robert Pace and Josephine Wolverton. By permission of D.C. Heath.

Macmillan Publishing Company
866 Third Avenue
New York, N.Y. 10022

Printed in the United States of America

ISBN: 0-02-295001-X
9 8 7 6 5 4 3

PHOTOGRAPHY

AUTHORS

Barbara Staton has taught music at all levels, kindergarten through college, and for eight years was music television teacher for the State of Georgia. She is author of a four-volume series of books and records designed to teach music concepts through movement. She holds a B.S. degree in Music Education and an M.A. in Dance and Related Arts. Mrs. Staton has written numerous songs for television and recordings and is a composer member of ASCAP.

Dr. Merrill Staton earned his M.A. and Ed.D. degrees from Teachers College, Columbia University, and is nationally known as a music educator, choral conductor, singer, ASCAP composer, and record producer. He has been music director of and has conducted the Merrill Staton Voices on many network TV series and recordings. Dr. Staton has been a leader in the field of music education for over thirty years, and pioneered the use of children's voices on recordings for education.

Marilyn Copeland Davidson has taught music for over thirty years at all levels and is presently teaching elementary general music in Pequannock, New Jersey. She also teaches graduate music education courses. She holds a B.S. degree from Ball State University in Muncie, Indiana, a diploma from the Juilliard School of Music, and has completed the Master Class level of Orff-Schulwerk. She has served as national vice-president and president of the American Orff-Schulwerk Association.

Dr. Phyllis Kaplan, Coordinator of Elementary General Music for the Montgomery County public schools in Rockville, Maryland, received her Ph.D. in Music Education from the University of Michigan. She has taught in the Ohio public schools and at Kent State and Penn State universities. She has served on the MENC National Committee on Music Education for Handicapped Learners and the editorial board of the *Music Educators Journal.* Dr. Kaplan is currently president-elect of the Maryland Music Education Association.

Dr. Susan Snyder has taught general music for over twenty years. She holds a Ph.D. in Curriculum and Instruction and an Orff Master Teacher's Certificate. She has worked with preschool and handicapped children and has done extensive study in aesthetics, early childhood, and the Kodály approach. Currently, Dr. Snyder is teaching in the Greenwich, Connecticut, public schools. She is an adjunct faculty member of Teachers College, Columbia University, and Director of the Ridgewood Summer Courses, Ridgewood, New Jersey.

SPECIAL CONTRIBUTORS

Dr. Betty Atterbury
Mainstreaming

Marshia Beck
Movement

Mary Frances Early
African American Music

Joan Gregoryk
Vocal Development

János Horváth
Kodály

Virginia Mead
Dalcroze

Mollie Tower
Listening Selections

CONSULTANTS AND CONTRIBUTING WRITERS

Dr. Betty Atterbury
University of Southern Maine
Gorham, Maine

Marshia Beck
Holy Names College
Oakland, California

Diane Bennette
Bergenfield Public Schools
Bergenfield, New Jersey

Dr. Joyce Boorman
University of Alberta
Edmonton, Alberta, Canada

Teri Burdette
Barnsley Elementary
Rockville, Maryland

Dr. Robert A. Duke
University of Texas
Austin, Texas

Mary Frances Early
Atlanta Public Schools
Atlanta, Georgia

Nancy Ferguson
University of Arizona
Tucson, Arizona

Diane Fogler
Rockaway Township Public Schools
Rockaway, New Jersey

Joan Gregoryk
Chevy Chase Elementary
Chevy Chase, Maryland

János Horváth
University of Calgary
Calgary, Alberta, Canada

Dr. Judith A. Jellison
University of Texas
Austin, Texas

Dr. JaFran Jones
Bowling Green State University
Bowling Green, Ohio

James Kenward
Howe Avenue Elementary
Sacramento, California

Tom Kosmala
Pittsburgh Public Schools
Pittsburgh, Pennsylvania

Virginia Mead
Kent State University
Kent, Ohio

Jane Pippart
Lancaster Public Schools
Lancaster, Pennsylvania

Belle San Miguel-Ortiz
San Antonio Independent School
District, San Antonio, Texas

Mollie Tower
Austin Independent School District
Austin, Texas

contents

UNIT 1 SOUNDS AROUND US

BEATS

What are some ways to keep the beat?

● Listen to these city sounds.

 "City Sounds"

● Say hello to your friends with this song.

Hello, There!

Traditional

Hel - lo, there! (Hel - lo, there!) How are you? (How are you?)

It's so good (It's so good) To see you. (To see you.)

We'll sing and (We'll sing and) be hap - py (be hap - py)

That we're all here to - geth - er a - gain!

HIGH AND LOW

 Sing about our country.

America

Music by Henry Carey
Words by Samuel F. Smith

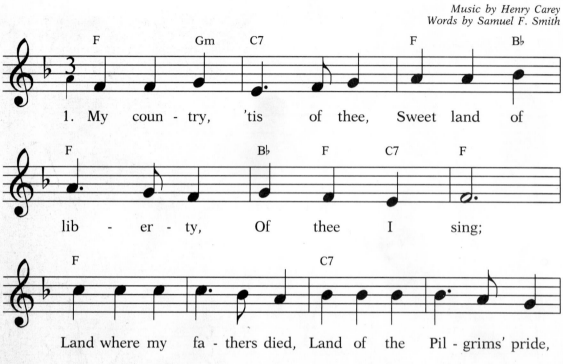

1. My coun - try, 'tis of thee, Sweet land of lib - er - ty, Of thee I sing; Land where my fa - thers died, Land of the Pil - grims' pride,

From ev - 'ry __ moun - tain - side Let __ free - dom ring.

2. Our father's God, to Thee, Author of liberty,
   To Thee we sing;
   Long may our land be bright With Freedom's holy light;
   Protect us by Thy might, Great God, our King!

Sounds can be **high** or **low**.

Pitch means how high or low a sound is.

● Listen for high and low pitches in "America."

Notes on a music **staff** show pitch.
Low pitches are shown lower on
the staff than higher pitches.
These are the lowest and highest
pitches in "America."

● Find the words in the song that
are sung on these pitches.

STEADY BEAT

These children are playing together in a park.

Music is part of their fun.

Old King Glory

Traditional

Old King Glo - ry of the moun - tain.

The moun - tain reached so high,

it near - ly reached the sky.

The first one, the sec - ond one, the third fol - low me.

PLAYING HIGH AND LOW

- Take turns playing this **pattern** on high and low C bells.

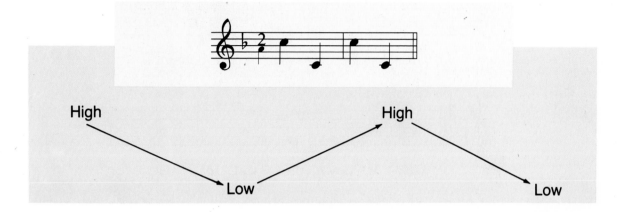

- Find a good place to play this pattern in "Old King Glory."

- Raise and lower your arms as you hear higher and lower sounds in this music.

 "The Aviary," from *The Carnival of the Animals* by Camille Saint-Saëns

SOUNDS OF TRAINS

Engine, Engine Number Nine

Traditional

so   En - gine, en - gine   num - ber   nine,

Go - ing   down   the   rail - road   line!

If   the   train   goes   off   the   track,

Will   I   get   my   mon - ey   back?

- Find lines of the song that look the same.
  Will they sound the same?
- Find the lower notes.
- Listen for higher and lower sounds in this music
  about a train ride.

 "The Little Train of the Caipira" from *Bachianas Brasileiras* No. 2, by Heitor Villa-Lobos

RHYTHM OF TRAINS

- As you sing, point to a car for each beat.

- Look at the notes on the train.

  Which beat has only one sound?

- Find this pattern in "Engine, Engine Number Nine."

● Ride the little train.

Station Number 2

Let off steam!

"We're all on our way . . .

"We're all on our way. . . .

Watch the bumps!

The train starts slowly.

Whistle!

Keep
braking

Station Number 1

Start ↑ here

10

This
way
first

City Limits

Start slowing down

Station Number 3

Stop

S–L–O–W–E–R

Let off steam!

11

Clickety Clack

Music by Hap Palmer
Words by Martha and Hap Palmer

Solo
Car - ry - ing lum - ber down the track; —

Group
Go - ing to the cit - y and it won't come — back.

Solo
Car - ry - ing coal down the track; —

Group
Go - ing to the cit - y and it won't come — back.

Solo
Car - ry - ing pro - duce down the track; —

Group
Go - ing to the cit - y and it won't come — back.

Car - ry - ing grain ___ down the track; ___

Go - ing to the cit - y and it won't come ___ back.

Refrain

All

Woo, woo, click - e - ty clack,

This old train ___ is ___ load - ed down. ___

Woo, woo, click - e - ty clack,

This old train ___ is ___ cit - y bound. ___

13

RHYTHM OF RAIN

You can help tell this story.

You will make the sound of the rain.

A Wish Comes True

John woke up one Saturday morning.

He could hear something hitting the roof.

It sounded like this:

"Oh, no," said John,

"I know what that sound is.

"It's starting to rain.

"What will happen to my baseball game?"

The rain was now dripping with a very steady beat.

John sang along with the rain. These are the pitches he sang.

Rain, rain, go a-way. Come a-gain an-oth-er day.

Then the raindrops started to fall more often.

Now they sounded like this:

John sang more of the song:

Rain, rain, go a-way. All the chil-dren want to play.

"It's fun to sing with the rain," said John.

"Now, I wish it would stop.

Then we could play our game today. I

know! I'll make up a **verse**!"

I wish the rain would stop! Ev-'ry sin-gle drip-py drop!

Just then he heard:

Then he heard:

Nothing! John heard nothing!

John could hardly believe it!

He had gotten his wish!

● Listen and move to the music. Pretend you are

plants in the rain.

 "Gardens in the Rain," by Claude Debussy

SOUNDS AND SILENCES

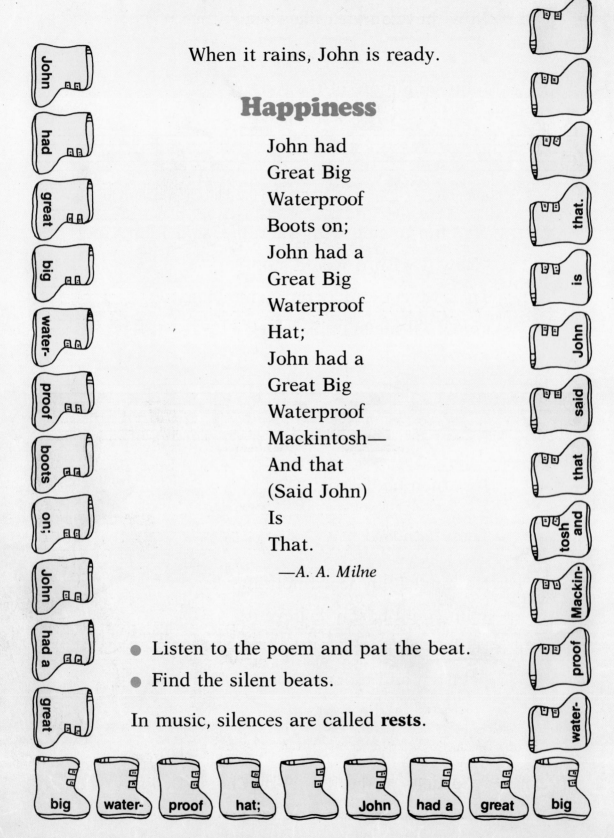

When it rains, John is ready.

Happiness

John had
Great Big
Waterproof
Boots on;
John had a
Great Big
Waterproof
Hat;
John had a
Great Big
Waterproof
Mackintosh—
And that
(Said John)
Is
That.
            —A. A. Milne

● Listen to the poem and pat the beat.
● Find the silent beats.

In music, silences are called **rests**.

- Listen for the silent beats in the music.
- Find the places in this song where your voice rests.

If You're Happy

Traditional

2. If you're happy and you know it, tap your foot.

3. If you're happy and you know it, nod your head.

4. If you're happy and you know it, do all three.

SINGING GAMES

Who Has the Penny?

Traditional

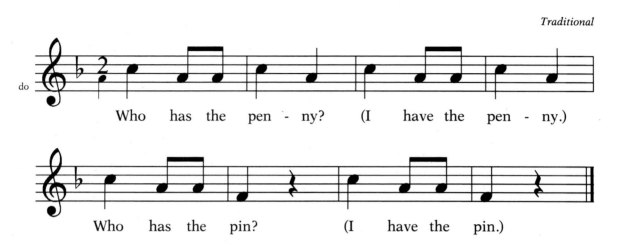

Who has the pen - ny? (I have the pen - ny.)

Who has the pin? (I have the pin.)

● Find a new pitch in this song.

Bow, Wow, Wow!

do

"Bow, wow, wow!"

"Whose dog art thou?"

"Lit - tle Tom - my Tuck - er's dog.

Bow, wow, wow!"

● Find the rests on the silent beats.

This music sign is one kind of rest: ξ

● Find the lines that are the same

as the rhythms in this box:

A TRIP AROUND THE CITY

Let's pretend to take a trip around the city.

- Look at the pictures on this page.

  They will make you think of songs you know.

20

JUST CHECKING

See how much you remember.

1. Are these rhythm patterns the same or different?

a.

b.

2. Which is the higher note?

a.

b.

3. Which rhythm pattern shows two sounds to a beat?

a.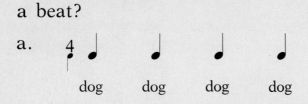

b.

4. Which music sign is a rest?

TWO WAYS OF SEEING A PICTURE

This is a photograph of a bridge.

The bridge is in a garden.

This is a painting of the same bridge.
This painting does not try to show the
bridge exactly.

Water Lilies and Japanese Bridge,
Claude Monet, MUSEUM OF FINE ARTS, Boston

TWO WAYS TO HEAR A STORY

Music cannot tell a story exactly.

It lets you picture the story inside your head.

● Listen to this music and picture the story that fits this music.

"Conversations of Beauty and the Beast" from
Mother Goose Suite, by Maurice Ravel

"Beauty and the Beast" takes place in a garden.

- Listen to the story.
- Listen to the music again.

UNIT 2 SOUNDS OF AUTUMN

PLAY INSTRUMENTS

membrane

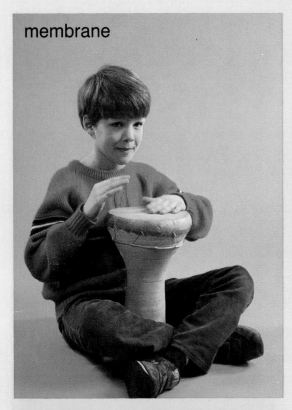

rattle

metal

wood

28

Autumn Woods

I like the woods
   in Autumn
When dry leaves hide the ground,
When the trees are bare
And the wind sweeps by
With a lonesome rushing sound.

I can rustle the leaves
   in Autumn
And I can make a bed
In the thick dry leaves
That have fallen
From the bare trees
Overhead.

—James S. Tippett

- Say the words of the rhythm.
- Choose one of the instruments you see and play this rhythm with the poem.

Au-tumn leaves fall

♪♪ are called **eighth notes.**

They show two sounds to a beat.

♩ is called a **quarter note.**

It shows one sound to a beat.

♩ is called a **quarter rest.**

It shows no sound for a beat.

The Witch Rides

Music by Grace M. Meserve
Verses 1 and 3 by Grace M. Meserve
Verses 2 and 4 by Mary Jaye

1. The witch is on her broom - stick
2.   See the ghosts come float - ing

Rid - ing ver - y fast,
White a - gainst the sky,

Oo - oo   Oo - oo
Oo - oo   Oo - oo

Hal - low - een at last. _____
They go drift - ing by. _____

3. The skeleton is dancing
   On his bony toes,
   Tipping, tapping,
   On and on he goes.

4. See the funny goblins
   Dancing down the street,
   Knocking, knocking,
   Crying "Trick or treat."

31

GETTING LOUDER
AND SOFTER

- Play Follow the Leader.
- Get louder as the leader's hands move apart.

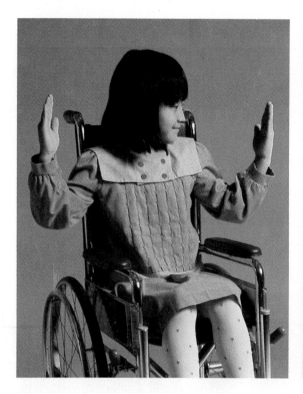 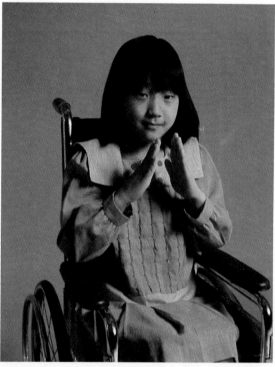

- Get softer as the leader's hands move close together.

These are two signs used in music.
They tell you when to get louder and when
to get softer.

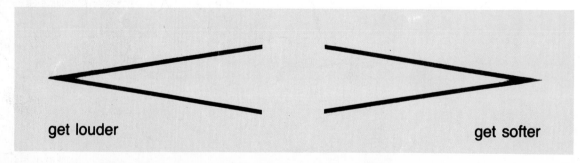

get louder   get softer

● Say each line, getting louder and getting softer.

2.

Mee - na dee - na, di - na duss,

Cat - a - la wee - na wi - na wuss.

Spit! Spot! Must be done!

Twid - dle - um, twad - dle - um, twen - ty - one!

maracas

tom-tom

rhythm sticks

cymbal

This picture is made from the music signs for getting louder and getting softer.

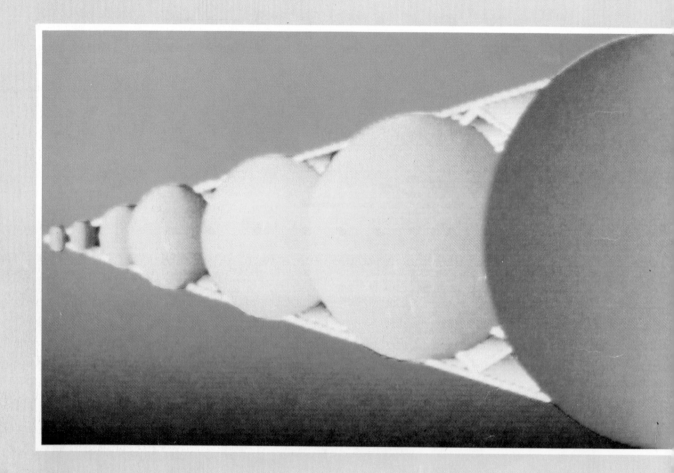

● Follow the picture with two fingers as you listen to "Bydlo."

 "Bydlo" ("The Ox-Cart") from *Pictures at an Exhibition,* by Modest Mussorgsky

RHYTHM PATTERNS

Hallowe'en

Grace C. Nash

1. Hal - low - e'en,   Hal - low - e'en,   Pump - kins   fat.
2. Hal - low - e'en,   Hal - low - e'en,   Ghost,   fly   high.

Hal - low - e'en,   Hal - low - e'en,   Pump - kins   fat.
Hal - low - e'en,   Hal - low - e'en,   Ghost,   fly   high.

Witch - es ride on   broom - sticks,   Wear - ing sau - cy   hats,
Gob - lins sit on   fen - ces,   Eat - ing pump - kin   pie,

Hal - low - e'en,   Hal - low - e'en,   Big   black   cats!
Hal - low - e'en,   Hal - low - e'en,   Ooh,   OH   MY!

● Say the rhythm of "Hallowe'en." Use these words
in place of the words in the song.

Say "creepy" when you see ♪♪

Say "ghost" when you see ♩

Say "ooh!" when you see ♩

Make no sound when you see 𝄽

In this song ♩ sounds for two beats.

How many different sounds can you hear when you
look at this painting?

A CANON

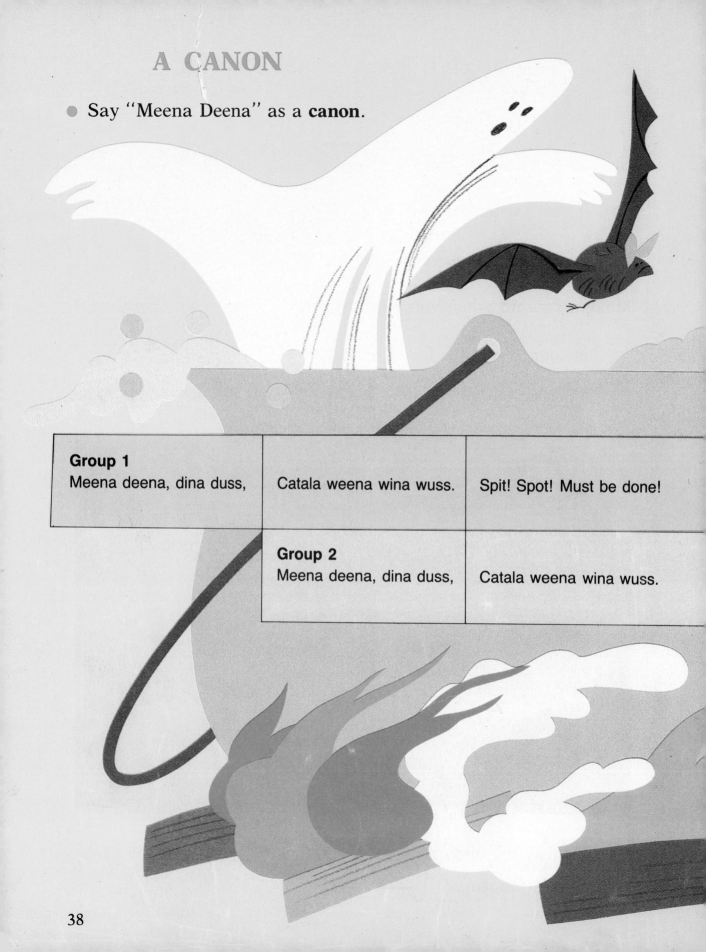

- Say "Meena Deena" as a **canon**.

Group 1 Meena deena, dina duss,	Catala weena wina wuss.	Spit! Spot! Must be done!
Group 2 Meena deena, dina duss,	Catala weena wina wuss.	

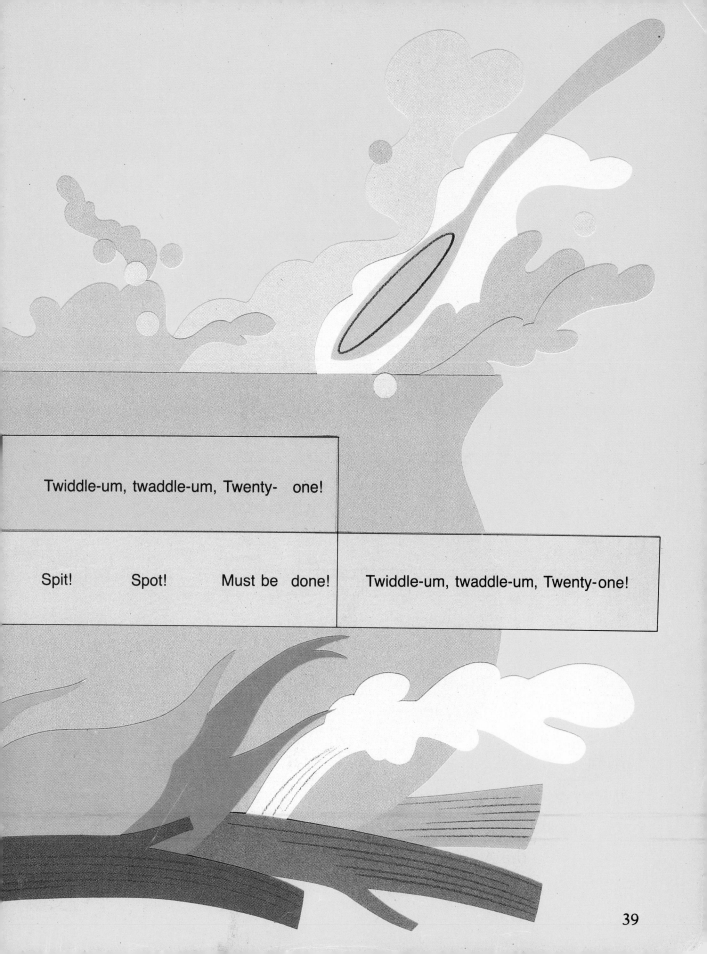

Twiddle-um, twaddle-um, Twenty- one!

Spit!   Spot!   Must be done!   Twiddle-um, twaddle-um, Twenty-one!

39

GUESS WHO?

False Face

Words by Susan Rupert
Music by David Russell

Who's be-hind this false face?   No-bod-y knows but me!

Who's be-hind this false face?   No-bod-y knows but me!

I   won't   tell   you,   You   will   have   to   guess;

Go back to the beginning and sing to the End.
(Da Capo al Fine)

If   our   guess is right,   You will an - swer, "Yes!"

Music can have more than one **section.**

The order of the sections is called **form.**

In this song the A section returns after the B section.

The form of this song is ABA.

- Say and play these ghostly rhythms.

- Play this rhythm as you sing the first part of "False Face."

You may want to get louder (——————)
or softer (============) as you play.

A SINGING GAME

Looby Loo

English Singing Game

With a swing

Here we go loo - by loo, Here we go loo - by light,

Here we go loo - by loo, All on a Hal - low - een night. —

1. I put my right hand in, — I take my right hand out, — I

Go back to the beginning and sing to the End.
(Da Capo al Fine)

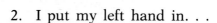

give my hand a shake, shake, shake, And turn my - self a - bout. Oh,

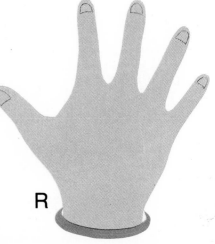

2. I put my left hand in. . .

3. I put my right leg in. . .

4. I put my left leg in. . .

5. (*Make up your own verse.*)

L   R

"Looby Loo" has two different sections (A and B).
Since the A section returns after the last B section,
the form is ABA.
This is what you do to show that you hear
each section.

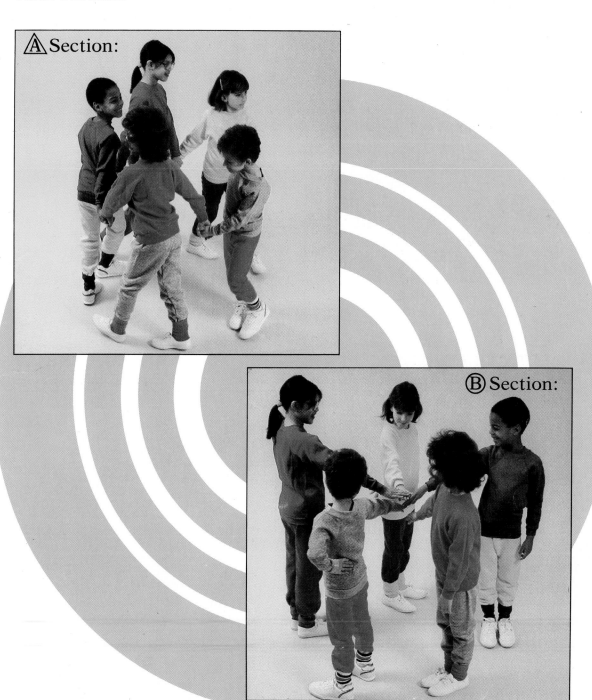

Ⓐ Section:

Ⓑ Section:

LET'S HAVE A HALLOWEEN PARTY!

These children are going to a Halloween party at this house.

Who else is coming to the party?

● Sing "The Witch Rides" as the children go to the house.

● Pretend you are stirring a witch's brew.

44

The Pumpkin in the Patch

Traditional Melody

1. The pump-kin in the patch, the pump-kin in the patch,

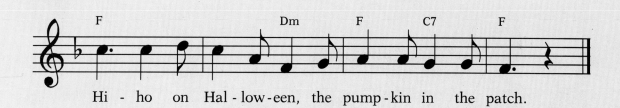

Hi - ho on Hal - low-een, the pump-kin in the patch.

 2. The pumpkin calls a witch. . .

 5. The ghost scares us all. . .

 3. The witch calls a bat. . .

 6. We all scare the ghost. . .

 4. The bat calls a ghost. . .

● Play a Halloween game.

● Sing the song together. Play this game the same
way that you play "The Farmer in the Dell."

● Choose a pumpkin to be "it."

45

JUST CHECKING

See how much you remember.

1. Name the family to which each instrument below belongs.

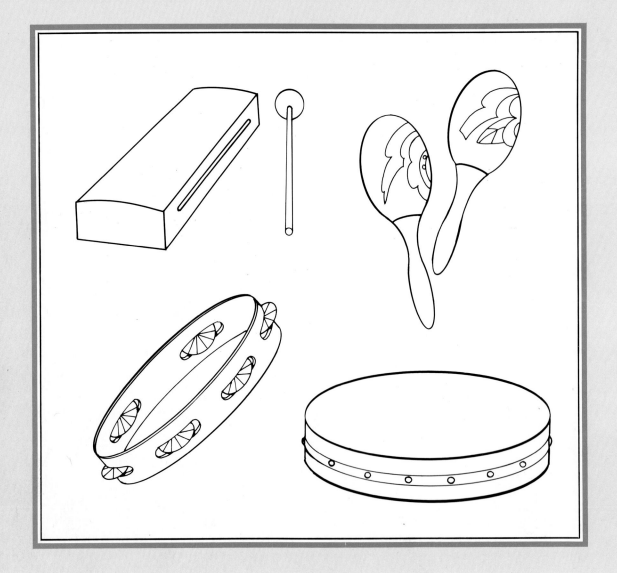

2. What family is missing?

3. Which music sign means no sound?

4. ABA is a form used in music.

   Name two songs you know that are in ABA form.

5. Which drawing shows ABA form?

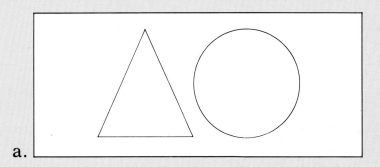

a.

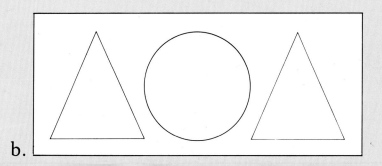

b.

UNIT 3 SOUNDS OF HARVEST

THANKSGIVING GREETINGS.

49

COUNTRY MUSIC

● Listen for these instruments in "Country Music"

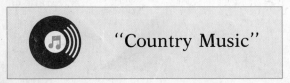

"Country Music"

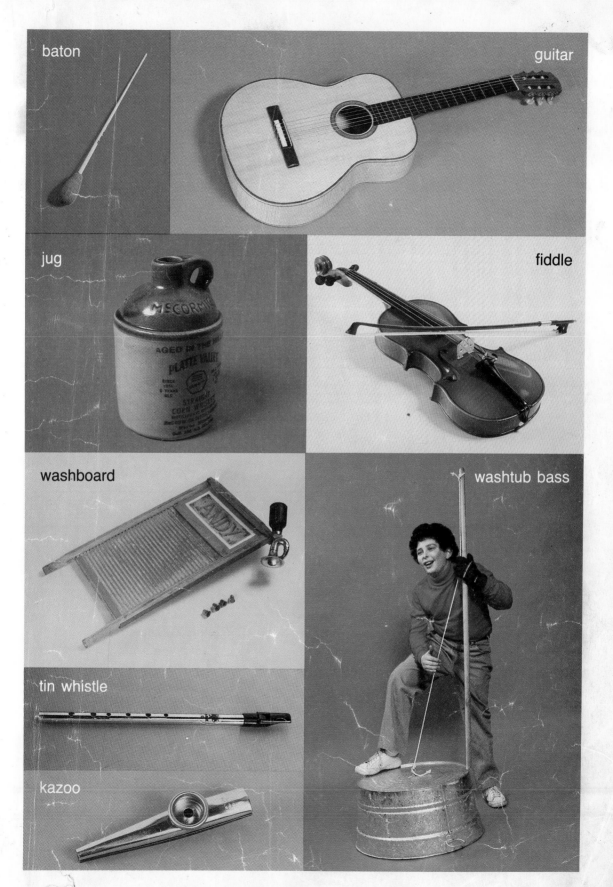

baton

guitar

jug

fiddle

washboard

washtub bass

tin whistle

kazoo

Each farm animal makes a different sound.

In this song, you will sing some animal sounds that
are *very* different.

Barnyard Song

Kentucky Mountain Song

1. I had a cat and the cat pleased me.

I fed my cat un - der yon - der tree.

Cat goes fid - dle - i - fee. _____

2. I had a hen and the hen pleased me.
   I fed my hen under yonder tree.
   Hen goes chimmy chuck, chimmy chuck,
   Cat goes fiddle-i-fee.

3. I had a duck and the duck pleased me.
   I fed my duck under yonder tree.
   Duck goes quack, quack,
   Hen goes chimmy chuck, chimmy chuck,
   Cat goes fiddle-i-fee.

4. I had a goose. . .
   Goose goes hissy, hissy. . .

5. I had a sheep. . .
   Sheep goes baa, baa. . .

6. I had a cow. . .
   Cow goes moo, moo. . .

7. I had a horse. . .
   Horse goes neigh, neigh. . .

52

Look at the instruments.

Each instrument makes a different sound.

How many of these instruments can you name?

 Listen for the sounds of these instruments.

Children's Symphony, third movement by Harl McDonald

LOUD AND SOFT
IN MUSIC

● Remember that this sign means the music should get louder.

Crescendo is a word that means to get louder.

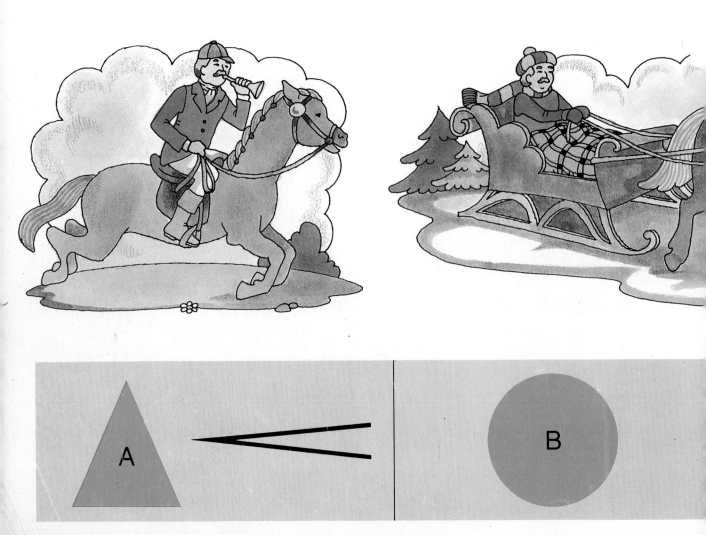

- Remember that this sign means the music should get softer.

Decrescendo is a word that means to get softer.

- Listen for a crescendo and a decrescendo in *Children's Symphony,* third movement, by Harl McDonald.

How Animals Sleep

Did you ever wonder how animals sleep—
Creatures that run and jump and leap?
The horse stands up, but not the cow,
And bugs and spiders? I don't know how!
A cat curls up in a warm, round ball,
A mouse nestles up in a hole in the wall.
Now, if you wonder how others doze,
You'll have to ask someone else who knows.

—*Peter Michaelson*

Bingo

Traditional Folk Melody

There was a farm-er had a dog, and Bin-go was his name-O

B - I - N-G-O, B - I - N-G-O,

B - I - N-G-O, and Bin-go was his name-O.

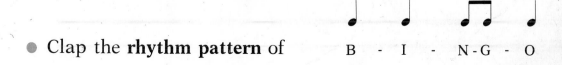

- Clap the **rhythm pattern** of   B - I - N-G-O

- Find the rhythm pattern in the song.

HARVESTING RHYTHMS

● Think of ways to act out this song.

Harvest

Danish Folk Song
Words Adapted

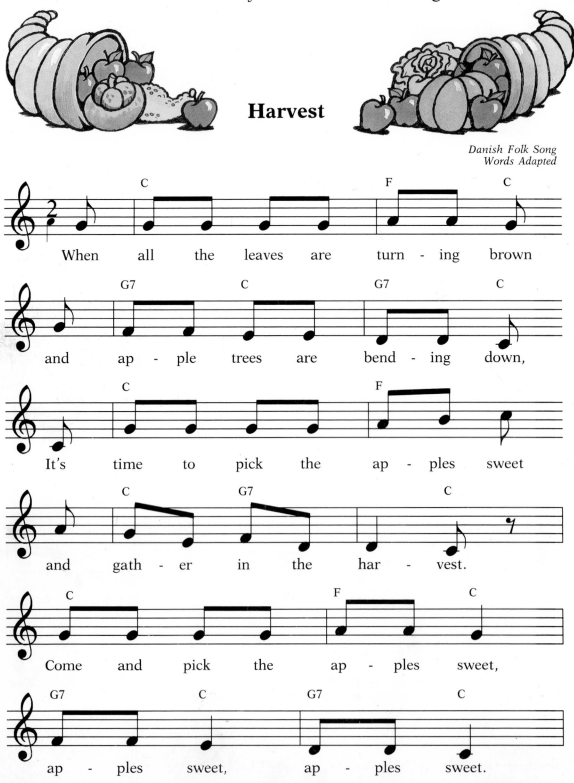

When all the leaves are turn - ing brown

and ap - ple trees are bend - ing down,

It's time to pick the ap - ples sweet

and gath - er in the har - vest.

Come and pick the ap - ples sweet,

ap - ples sweet, ap - ples sweet.

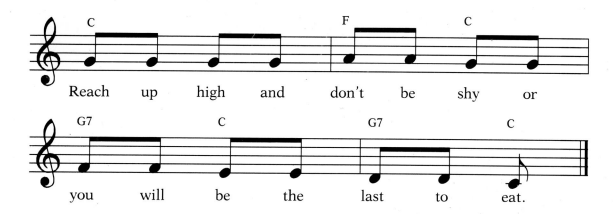

Reach   up   high   and   don't   be   shy   or

you   will   be   the   last   to   eat.

● Use names of fruit and vegetables to read this rhythm. Hold the word *squash* for two beats.

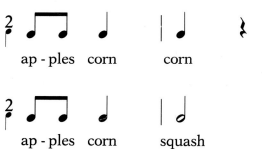

ap - ples corn   corn

ap - ples corn   squash

● Read these rhythm patterns using the names again.

1.

2.

3.

Which rhythm pattern did you clap in "Bingo"?

A FAVORITE
COUNTRY SONG

She'll Be Comin' Round the Mountain

Southern Mountain Song

1. She'll be com-in' round the moun-tain when she comes,
2. She'll be driv-in' six white hor-ses when she comes,

She'll be com-in' round the moun-tain when she comes,
She'll be driv-in' six white hor-ses when she comes,

She'll be com-in' round the moun-tain,
She'll be driv-in' six white hor-ses,

She'll be com-in' round the moun-tain,
She'll be driv-in' six white hor-ses,

She'll be com-in' round the moun-tain when she comes.
She'll be driv-in' six white hor - ses when she comes.

3. Oh, we'll all go out to meet her when she comes. . .

4. Oh, we'll all have chicken and dumplings when she comes. . .

5. She will have to sleep with Grandma when she comes. . .

● Use fruit or vegetable names to say these rhythm patterns.

● Read these rhythm patterns as a canon. Do you remember a song that has these rhythm patterns?

What do you see in this picture?
How many kinds of fruits and vegetables can you name?

L'Autunno, Giuseppe Arcimboldo, PINACOTECA CIVICA, Brescia

INDIANS AT
HARVEST TIME

● Read this American Indian poem.

A Tuscarora Indian Poem
My children, take this gift.
In love do I bestow it,
And in love shall you receive it.
It will feed you and sustain you.
It will prosper you and keep you.
Through this gift of corn I bring
All your children will be blessed—
Only live in peace and friendship.
Live in friendship with each other.

Tuscarora Corn Husk Doll
© Pres. & Fellows of Harvard College 1986,
PEABODY MUSEUM, HARVARD UNIVERSITY,
Photograph by Hillel Burger.

This sand painting was made
by a Navajo Indian man.
He drew the picture using
sand and colored rock. He
believed the painting would
help make sick people well.

Sandpainting Demonstration MUSEUM OF NORTH ARIZONA, Flagstaff

This is a song of the Navajo Indians.

The Navajo live in the southwestern United States.

Navajo Happy Song

Traditional Navajo

When beats are grouped in sets of two, the first
beat is the stronger beat.

In this song, the notes on the **strong beat** are
marked.

Over the River and Through the Wood

Traditional Melody
Words by Lydia Maria Childs

1. O - ver the riv - er and through the wood,
2. O - ver the riv - er and through the wood,

To grand - moth - er's house we go; _____
Trot fast _____ my dap - ple gray! _____

The horse knows the way to car - ry the sleigh
Spring o - ver the ground like a hunt - ing hound, _

Through the white and drift - ed snow. _____
_ For this is Thanks - giv - ing day! _____

O - ver the riv - er and through the wood,
O - ver the riv - er and through the wood,

Oh, how the wind does blow! _____
Now grand - moth - er's face I spy! _____

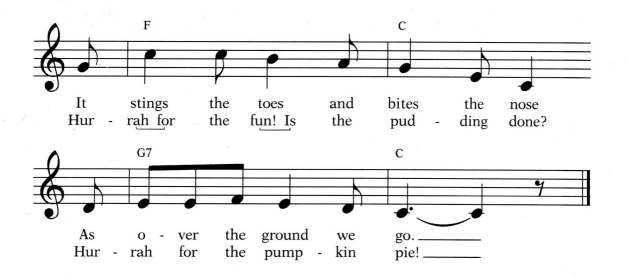

It stings the toes and bites the nose
Hur - rah for the fun! Is the pud - ding done?

As o - ver the ground we go.
Hur - rah for the pump - kin pie!

Over The River To Grandma's House On Thanksgiving Day, Grandma Moses.
copyright © 1979, Grandma Moses Properties Co., NY

● Look at this picture.

Where might you find such a scene?

PAT THE
STRONG BEAT

● Find the words that **rhyme**.

Five Fat Turkeys

Traditional

Five fat tur-keys are we,_____

We slept all night in a tree._____

When the cook came a-round we could-n't be found,

So that's why we're here, you see._____

● Say the words and clap the rhythm.

Travel Rhythms

1. Sing a - bout a   horse,
2. Clap   it with your hands,

Sing a - bout a   sleigh,
Stamp it with your feet,

Sing a - bout the   an - i - mals and
Find a way to   clap and say the

Thanks - giv - ing   day.
Rhythm   and the   beat.

GOING TO
GRANDMOTHER'S HOUSE

- Follow the path to Grandmother's house.
  The horse knows the way.

- Stop at each picture and sing the song that
  matches that picture.

70

JUST CHECKING

1. Match.

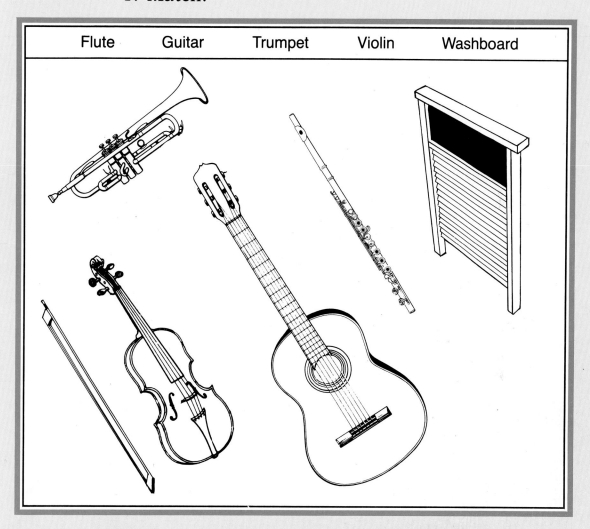

| Flute | Guitar | Trumpet | Violin | Washboard |

2. Which word tells you to get louder?

crescendo   decrescendo

3. Point to the notes that are on the strong beat.

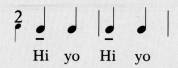

Hi yo Hi yo

UNIT 4

SOUNDS OF HOLIDAYS

LOW, MIDDLE, AND HIGH

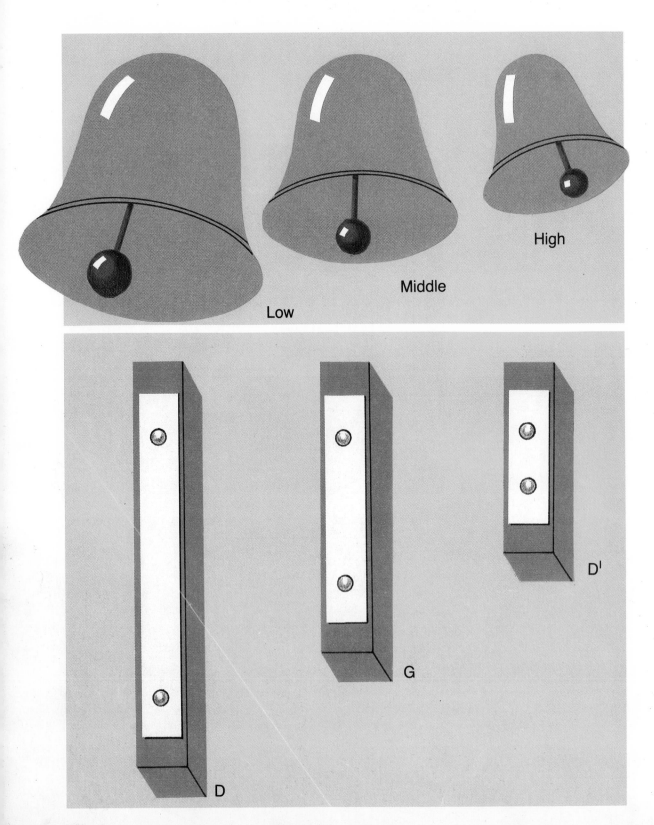

Low

Middle

High

D

G

D'

Small bells sound higher than large bells.

● Point to the highest sounding bell.

● Listen to the sounds of bells.

"Bells"

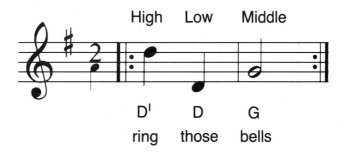

High   Low   Middle

D'   D   G

ring those bells

● Play this pattern four times on the bells.
Start softly, and then get louder,
making a crescendo.
Start loudly, and then get softer,
making a decrescendo.

Two kinds of bells are used in this song.

- Play the bell pattern on page 75 before and after you sing the song.
- Play jingle bells on the refrain.

Jingle Bells

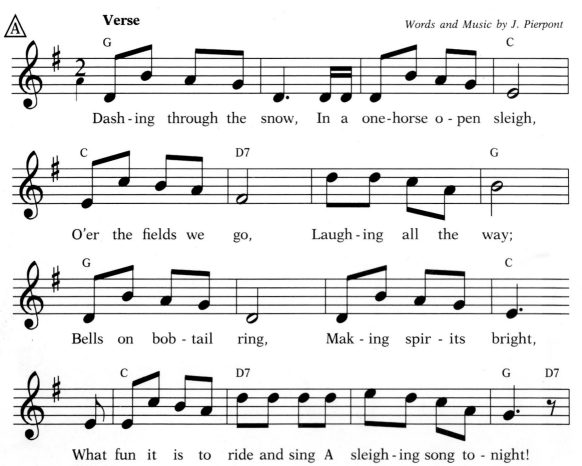

Words and Music by J. Pierpont

Verse

Dash-ing through the snow, In a one-horse o-pen sleigh,

O'er the fields we go, Laugh-ing all the way;

Bells on bob-tail ring, Mak-ing spir-its bright,

What fun it is to ride and sing A sleigh-ing song to-night!

Refrain

Jin-gle bells, jin-gle bells, jin-gle all the way!

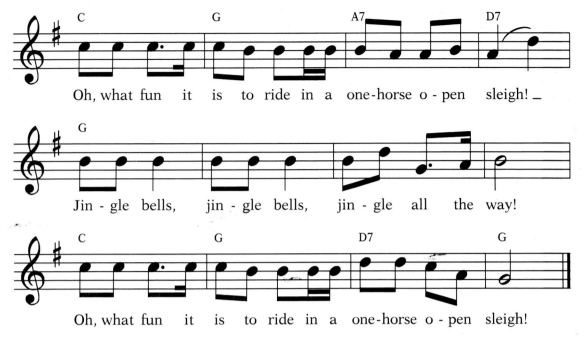

Oh, what fun it is to ride in a one-horse o-pen sleigh! _

Jin - gle bells, jin - gle bells, jin - gle all the way!

Oh, what fun it is to ride in a one-horse o-pen sleigh!

Horses pulling sleighs often wore small bells.

These bells were called sleigh bells.

ABA FORM

rattles · metals · woods · membranes

● Choose an instrument to play in the A sections.

● Choose an instrument from another family to play in the B section.

● Play the instruments for each word or group of words shown below.

● Play these instruments when you hear the same words in "A Time for Love."

A | ho ho ho · love · lots of snow · love

B | sing "joy"

A | ho ho ho · love · lots of snow · love

● Sing or play the notes between these
repeat signs ‖: :‖ again.

A Time for Love

Adapted from Nancy Dervan

De - cem - ber is a time for "ho ho ho," ___

De - cem - ber is a time for love. _____

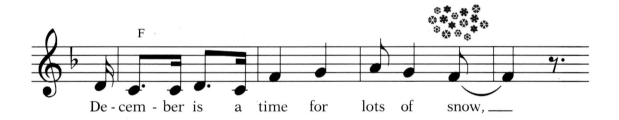

De - cem - ber is a time for lots of snow, ___

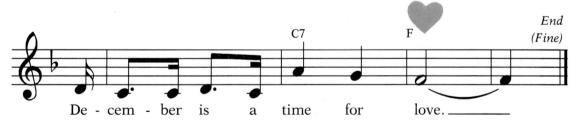

De - cem - ber is a time for love. _____

Go back to the beginning and sing to the end.
(Da Capo al Fine)

Sing "joy" ___ sing "joy" ___ Let ev - 'ry - one sing "joy." ___

A and B sections are found in this song about
Hanukah. What is the form?

● Pat the strong beat.

● Step on the strong beat.

Hanukah Song

Traditional
Words by Sue Snyder

Come see the lights, eight days and nights,
We will re - mem - ber on Ha - nu - kah.
From days of old, sto - ries are told,
We will re - mem - ber on Ha - nu - kah.
In the an - cient days of Is - ra - el
On - ly one cup of oil for light.

80

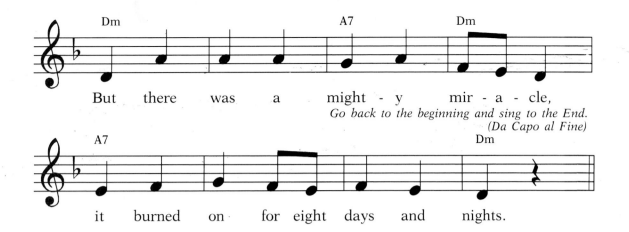

But there was a might - y mir - a - cle,

Go back to the beginning and sing to the End.
(Da Capo al Fine)

it burned on for eight days and nights.

Hanukah Oil Lamp. JEWISH MUSEUM, NY

If you step the strong beat in this song, you are stepping half notes. A **half note** (♩) lasts for two beats.

CRESCENDO AND
DECRESCENDO

A la Puerta del Cielo

Spanish Folk Song

A   la puer-ta   del   cie-lo   ven-den   za-pa-tos,
At   the gate of   Heav'n   lit-tle   shoes they   are   sell - ing,

Pa-ra los an-ge-li-tos que an-dan des-cal-zos.
For the lit-tle   bare-foot-ed   an-gels there dwell - ing.

Duer-me-te,   ni-ño,   Duer-me-te,   ni-ño,
Slum-ber, my   ba-by,   Slum-ber,   my   ba - by,

Duer-me-te,   ni-ño, a-rru,   a-rru.
Slum-ber, my   ba-by, a-rru,   a-rru.

- Follow the signs ⬿ and ⬾ with two fingers as you sing "A la Puerta del Cielo."
- Point to an angel on each strong beat as you softly sing the third line.

crescendo   decrescendo

What does each child want?

Jolly Old Saint Nicholas

Traditional Carol

1. Jol-ly old Saint Nich-o-las, Lean your ear this way!

Don't you tell a sin-gle soul What I'm going to say;

Christ-mas Eve is com-ing soon; Now, you dear old man,

Whis-per what you'll bring to me, Tell me, if you can.

2. When the clock is striking twelve
When I'm fast asleep,
Down the chimney broad and black,
With your pack you'll creep.
All the stockings you will find,
Hanging in a row,
Mine will be the shortest one,
You'll be sure to know.

3. Johnny wants a pair of skates,
Susie wants a sled,
Nellie wants a storybook,
One she hasn't read.
Now I think I'll leave to you
What to give the rest,
Choose for me, dear Santa Claus,
What you think is best.

84

- Read each Jolly Rhythm with the words.
- Say the rhythm patterns in order three times,
  using a decrescendo each time.

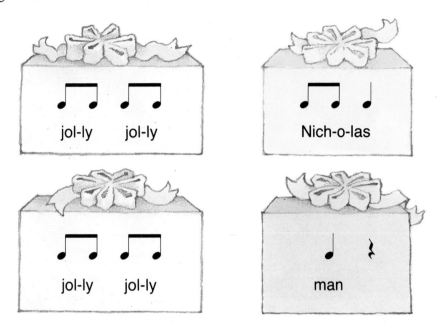

jol-ly   jol-ly

Nich-o-las

jol-ly   jol-ly

man

HALF NOTES

A note in this song that sounds for two beats
is called a **half note** (𝅗𝅥).

𝅗𝅥 sounds as long as ♩ ♩

● Find the half notes in this song.

What You Gonna Call Your Pretty Little Baby?

A **Refrain**

African American Spiritual

What you gon - na call your pret - ty lit - tle ba - by,

What you gon - na call your pret - ty lit - tle ba - by,

What you gon - na call your pret - ty lit - tle ba - by,

End (Fine)

Born, born in Beth - le - hem?

B **Verse**

1. Some say one thing, I'll say Im - man - u - el,

Go back to the beginning and sing to the end.
(Da Capo al Fine)

Born, born in Beth - le - hem.

2. Sweet little baby, Born in a manger,
  Born, born in Bethlehem.
  Refrain

● Pretend to rock a baby slowly from side to side as you sing.

● Rock to each side for two beats.

The Cradle, Berthe Morisot. JEU DE PAUME, Paris

A AND B SECTIONS IN
THE NUTCRACKER

Come to a party at Clara's house.

Clara is given a present.
It is a funny-looking nutcracker.
Clara likes it.

● Listen to the music and pretend

you are at Clara's party.

 "Miniature Overture" from *The Nutcracker* by
Peter Ilyich Tchaikovsky

ABA FORM IN
THE NUTCRACKER

The party at Clara's house is over.

Now it is night. Everyone has gone to sleep.

The nutcracker and the toy soldiers come to life.

● As you listen to "March," point to each beat of
the A section.

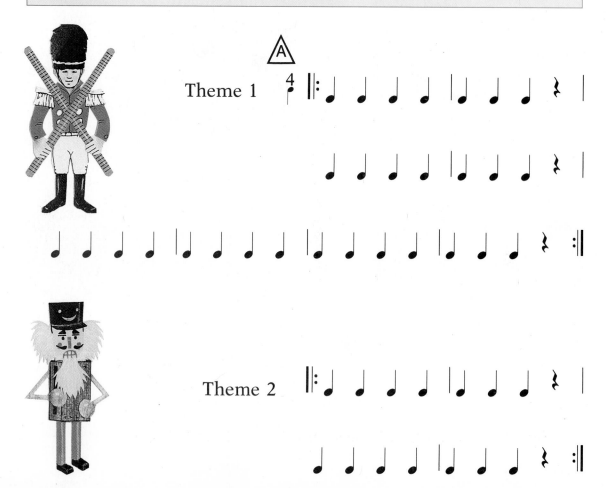

"March" from *The Nutcracker* by Peter Ilyich
Tchaikovsky

Theme 1

B Mouse part. Let your fingers be the mice.

A Then go back to the beginning and play to the End.

● Play rhythm sticks with Theme 1. Play a wood block with Theme 2. Shake jingle bells with the B section.

Clara wakes up and goes to visit the nutcracker.

The mice come out.

The nutcracker and the toys fight with the mice.

Clara saves the nutcracker from the Mouse King.

The nutcracker turns into a prince.

He takes Clara to a magic kingdom.

The Sugar Plum Fairy welcomes Clara and the prince to the magic kingdom.

- Listen for the celesta. The celesta looks like a piano but sounds like little bells.
- Listen for the sudden loud sounds played on the strings in the B section.

 "Dance of the Sugar Plum Fairy" from *The Nutcracker* by Peter Ilyich Tchaikovsky

● Follow the sections as you listen to this music in ABA form.

We Wish You a Merry Christmas

Traditional English Carol

1. We wish you a mer - ry Christ - mas,
We wish you a mer - ry Christ - mas.
We wish you a mer - ry Christ - mas,
And a hap - py New Year.

2. Now bring us some figgy pudding, (*3 times*)
And bring it out here.

3. For we love our figgy pudding, (*3 times*)
So bring some out here.

4. We won't go until we get some, (*3 times*)
So bring some out here.

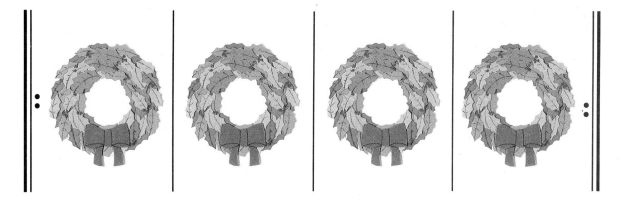

- Point to a bow on each <u>strong</u> beat.
- Play a triangle on the strong beat and let it ring
  until the next strong beat.

A TIME FOR GOOD CHEER

- Sing songs that make December special.
- Move to or play with the music.

JUST CHECKING

See how much you remember.

1. To which family of classroom instruments do these instruments belong?

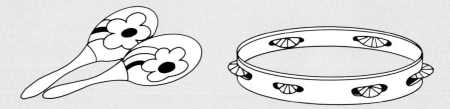

2. Point to the note that has the longer sound.

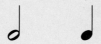

3.  sounds as long as which group of notes below?

4. Point to the musical form in which the first section is heard again at the end.

A B   A B A

5. Which sign tells you to get softer?

a.   b.

In this play, two of Santa's elves, Ho and Hum, find out what makes this time of year so special.

A Tale of TWO ELVES

by Deborah Goodell

CAST

Ho, one of Santa's elves
Hum, another elf
First Elf
Second Elf

Three Reindeer
Santa Claus
Other Elves
Singers and Dancers

(The elves are busy making toys at their tables. They have been working very hard for a long time. They are tired.)

(The elves say the words in rhythm as Ho and Hum start talking.)

98

HO: I'm so tired. All we do is work, work, work.

HUM: Me, too. I'm not making any more toys.

(The other elves stop working.)

FIRST ELF: But you're not finished!

HUM: I don't care. Santa will never miss one sled.

HO: Or these skates. Let's do something for fun.

HUM: I know! Let's go for a ride in Santa's sleigh!

HO: Great idea! I'm going with you.

SECOND ELF: You two go. But we're going to finish
our work.

(Ho and Hum get up and walk away. They start to sing.)

HO AND HUM:

Christ-mas time   go a-way, San-ta's hel-pers want to play.

(Ho and Hum walk along until they find Santa's
sleigh and three reindeer.)

HO: Reindeer, will you give us a sleigh ride?

REINDEER: We can give you a short ride.

HUM: Where are your bells?

REINDEER: Here they are. (They hold up their bells as
they stand up.)

(Ho and Hum climb into the sleigh. They sing "Ring those bells!" four times as the reindeer play D¹ D G on their bells.)

HO AND HUM: Here we go!

(Everyone sings "Jingle Bells." The reindeer prance as Ho and Hum jump up and down in their seats. Ho and Hum look around inside the sleigh.)

HO: Look, Hum. This must be Santa's magic TV. (Ho holds up the TV.) He sees if children are being good.

HUM: And this must be Santa's magic radio. (Hum holds up the radio.) He uses it to hear all the children's secret wishes.

(Ho and Hum turn on the TV.)

HO: Look! Those children are singing in Spanish to their baby brother.

(Children sing "A la Puerta del Cielo." Ho begins to fall asleep. Hum looks at Ho.)

HUM: Ho, don't fall asleep now! (Hum looks at the TV.) Here comes another picture. The children are singing and dancing for Hanukah. Look at all the fun they're having.

(Children sing "Hanukah Song," and dance.)

HO: Don't stop! We're having so much fun! Stay, Hanukah!

HUM: It's no use, Ho. Our picture has changed. Now it shows children singing Christmas carols. (Children sing "What You Gonna Call Your Pretty Little Baby?" and "We Wish You a Merry Christmas," and then leave.)

HO: Don't go away! Oh, Please stay, Christmas!

HUM: Sorry, Ho. They're gone. (Hum looks at the TV.) Here are children gathering around someone.

HO: It's Santa! The children are whispering to him.

HUM: We'll have to turn on this magic radio to hear their wishes.

(Ho and Hum turn on the radio and listen.)

(Children sing "Jolly Old Saint Nicholas." Ho and Hum look at each other.)

HUM: Ho, did you hear what those children wanted?

HO: Yes! Johnny wants a pair of skates, and Susie wants a sled. We'd better get back to work. I never finished the skates!

HUM: And I never finished the sled. (Hum calls to the reindeer.) We have to get back. Santa's counting on us.

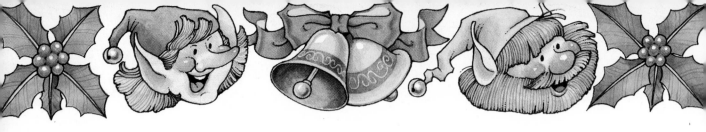

(Everyone sings the refrain of "Jingle Bells." Ho and Hum climb out of the sleigh.)

HO AND HUM: Thank you, reindeer. We loved your bells and our sleigh ride.

Ho and Hum say this poem as they walk back to the other elves.

Stay, Christmas!

Stay, Christmas!
Stay, Christmas!
Do not go
Away, Christmas.
Laughter jolly,
Lanterns, holly,
Bells ringing,
Children singing,
All things glad
Nothing sad . . .
Oh, Stay, Christmas!
Stay, Christmas.
Do not go
Away, Christmas.
   —Ivy O. Eastwick

FIRST ELF (to Ho and Hum): Are you the same elves who just a short while ago were singing "Christmas time, stay away"?

SECOND ELF: Why did you change your minds?

HO: We found Santa's TV and radio. When we turned them on, we saw children singing, and playing, and dancing.

HUM: And then we heard them whisper their secret wishes to Santa Claus. Lots of children are counting on Santa Claus. Santa Claus is counting on us!

HO AND HUM: We want to help make this time of year special.

SANTA CLAUS (coming in on the last line): And you have! As always, you have all my presents ready! I came to thank you, elves. (He turns to Ho and Hum.) And I'm glad you looked at my TV. Now you know why the children and I love December so much. (He holds out his arms to the children.)

(Everyone stands up and sings "A Time for Love.")

UNIT 5 SOUNDS OF WINTER

Sledding

Down the hill we're sliding,
Now's the time for play;
Frost is in the air,
It's a cold and wintry day.

We'll climb up and go again,
Down the hill we go;
Laughing as we're sliding,
And tumbling in the snow.

One more time we're flying,
One more faster run;
We can't wait for winter time
'Cause sledding is such fun.

—*M. S.*

● Listen for the sounds of winter in "Sleigh Ride."

 "Sleigh Ride" by Leroy Anderson

When the air is cold,
a bowl of hot soup tastes so good!

Chicken Soup with Rice

Music by Carole King
Words by Maurice Sendak

In Jan-u-ar-y it's so nice — while

slip-ping on the sli-ding — ice — to

sip hot chick-en soup with rice —

Sip-ping once — sip-ping twice —

sip-ping chick-en soup — with rice.

BEAT AND STRONG BEAT

● Say this word pattern with the song:

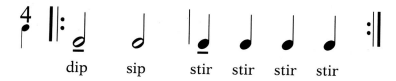

dip   sip   stir   stir   stir   stir

Set of beats are separated by a **bar line (|).**

● Find the bar line in the pattern above.

In this song the beats are in sets of four. The strong
beat is the first beat after each bar line.

● Find the bar lines in this song.

Which words will you sing on the strong beat?

Jim Along, Josie

American Folk Song

Ⓐ
C   G7   C

1. Hey, jim a - long, jim a - long, Jo - sie,

C   G7

Hey, jim a - long, jim a - long, Joe!

C   G7   C

Hey, jim a - long, jim a - long, Jo - sie,

C   G7   C   End (Fine)

Hey, jim a - long, jim a - long, Joe!

Ⓑ
C   (same words each time)   F   C

Face to the cen - ter, hands on your knees,

Go back to the beginning and sing to the End

F   C   F   C   G7   C   (Da Capo al Fine)

Clap three times and turn a - round, please!

2. Tiptoe along ...   4. Jump, jump along ...

3. Jog, jog along ...   5. Do what you want ...

110

PITCH IN MUSIC

Pitch is how high or low a sound is. The A section
of "Jim Along, Josie" uses five different pitches.

do
1

re
2

mi
3

so
5

la
6

Star Light, Star Bright

Traditional

Star light, Star bright, First star I see to-night, I wish I may I wish I might have the wish I wish to-night.

Coda

C	D	E	G	A
Hope	I	get	my	wish! _____

A **coda** is a short ending section.

● Play the coda on these bells.

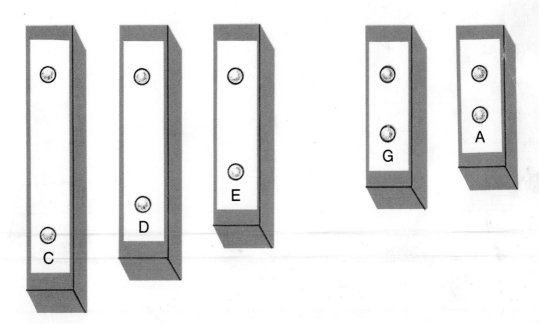

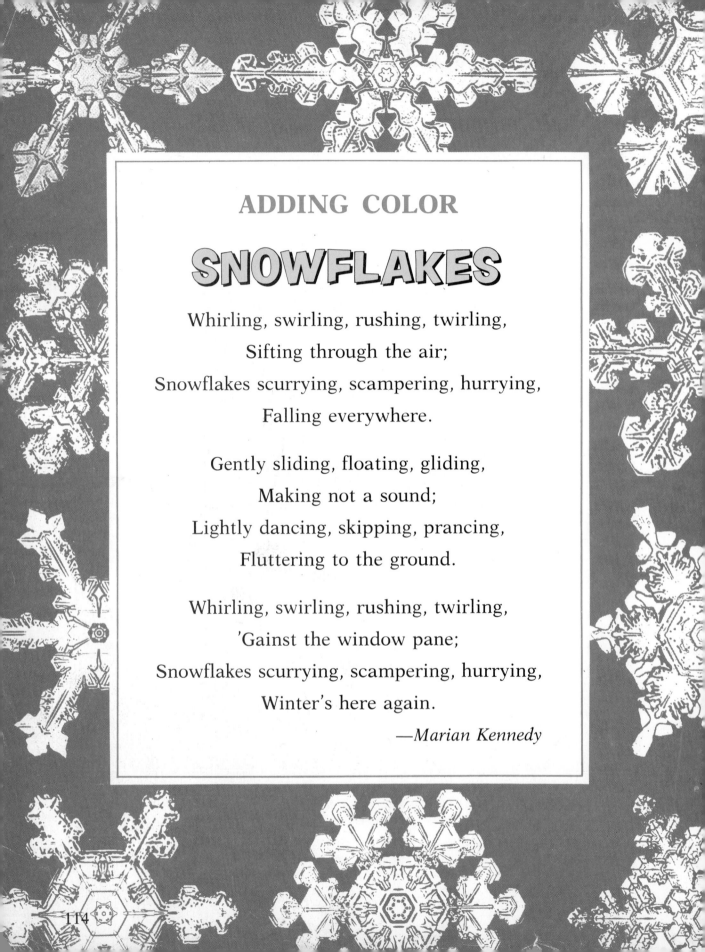

ADDING COLOR

SNOWFLAKES

Whirling, swirling, rushing, twirling,
Sifting through the air;
Snowflakes scurrying, scampering, hurrying,
Falling everywhere.

Gently sliding, floating, gliding,
Making not a sound;
Lightly dancing, skipping, prancing,
Fluttering to the ground.

Whirling, swirling, rushing, twirling,
'Gainst the window pane;
Snowflakes scurrying, scampering, hurrying,
Winter's here again.

—*Marian Kennedy*

115

Shake My Sillies Out

Music by Raffi
Words by Bert and Bonnie Simpson

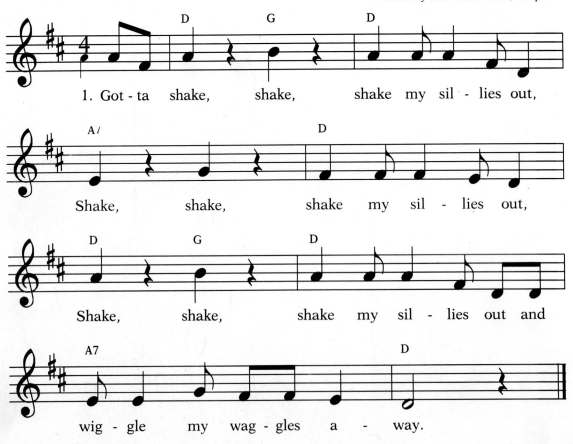

1. Got - ta shake, shake, shake my sil - lies out,
Shake, shake, shake my sil - lies out,
Shake, shake, shake my sil - lies out and
wig - gle my wag - gles a - way.

2. Gotta clap, clap, clap
my crazies out. . .
and wiggle my waggles away.

3. Gotta jump, jump, jump
my jiggles out. . .

4. (*slower*) Gotta yawn, yawn
yawn my sleepies out. . .

5. Gotta shake, shake, shake
my sillies out. . .

116

117

PHRASES

Martin Luther King

Words and Music by Teresa Fulbright

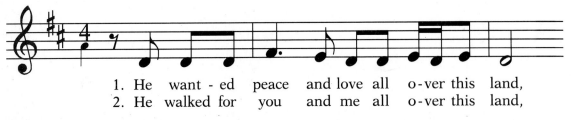

1. He want - ed peace and love all o - ver this land,
2. He walked for you and me all o - ver this land,

He want - ed peace and love all o - ver this land.
He walked for you and me all o - ver this land.

Mar - tin Lu - ther King was a peace lov - ing man.
Mar - tin Lu - ther King was a great, great ___ man,

He want - ed peace and love all o - ver this land.
He walked for you and me all o - ver this land.

3. He died for freedom's cause to save this land,
   He died for freedom's cause to save this land.
   Martin Luther King was a brave, brave man,
   He died for freedom's cause to save this land.

HAPPY RHYTHMS

The More We Get Together

German Folk Song

The more we get to-geth-er, to-geth-er, to-geth-er,

The more we get to-geth-er, the hap-pier we'll be!

For your friends are my friends, and my friends are your friends,

The more we get to-geth-er, the hap-pier we'll be!

120

- Choose a classroom instrument that can make a long sound.
- Play the instrument on the strong beat as you sing this song. Let it sound until the next strong beat.

The sound you will play is three beats long.

Each note below sounds for three beats.

The note for the sound looks like this: ♩.

It is called a **dotted half note.**

● Point to each dotted half note as you say "clown."

clown   clown   clown   clown

Each of these notes sounds for one beat.

● Point to each quarter note as you say "elephant."

el - e - phant   el - e - phant   el - e - phant   el - e - phant

● Read this rhythm using the words "elephant" and "clown."

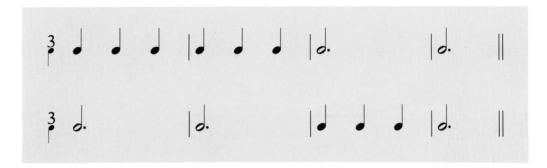

● Tap these rhythms with "Circus Music."

 "Circus Music" by Aaron Copland

Aaron Copland is a modern American composer.

He has written music in many styles.

His music often uses folk songs.

TIME FOR SKATING

Come Skating

They said come skating;

They said it's so nice.

They said come skating;

I'd done it twice.

They said come skating;

It sounded nice. . . .

I wore roller—

They meant ice.

—Shel Silverstein

(From A LIGHT IN THE ATTIC)

It's So Nice on the Ice

Richard M. Sherman
Robert B. Sherman

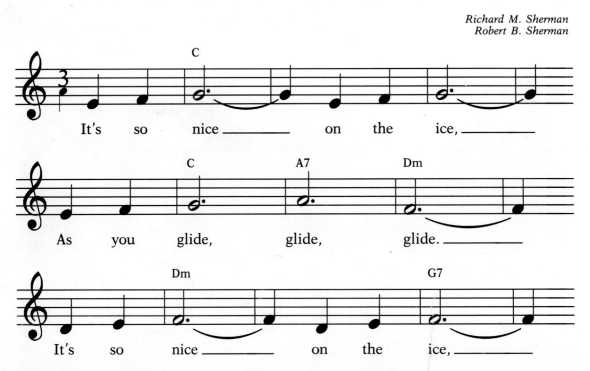

It's so nice _____ on the ice, _____

As you glide, glide, glide. _____

It's so nice _____ on the ice, _____

124

As you slide, slide, slide. _____

Come a - long, _____ come a - long, _____

Won't you try once or twice _____

And see how it feels to have wings on your heels?

It's so nice _____ on the ice. _____

"IT'S SO NICE ON THE ICE"
©Wonderland Music Co., Inc.
Words and Music by Richard M. and Robert B. Sherman

You can see **accents**.

● Look for accents.

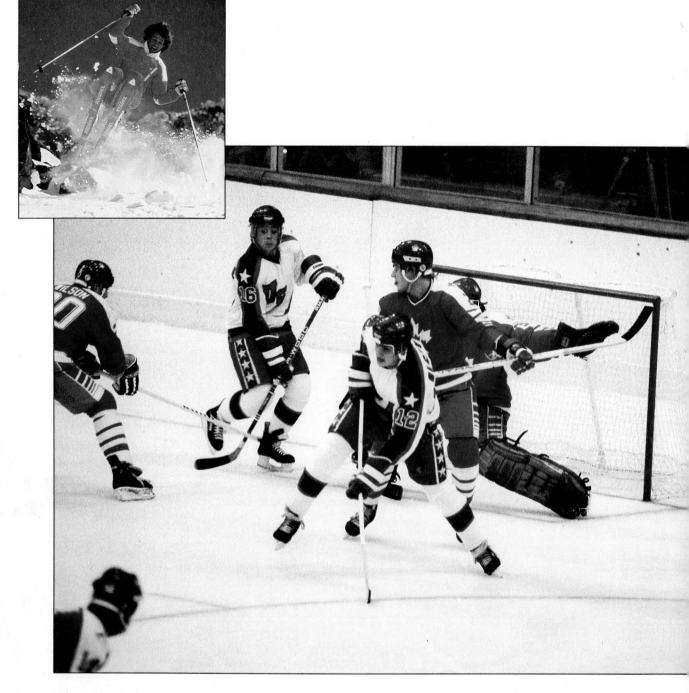

You can hear accents in music.

Accents are sudden louder sounds.

- Listen for accents at the start of this music.
- Move to the strong beat.

  Are the beats in sets of two or three?

 Waltz from *Les Patineurs,* by Giacomo Meyerbeer

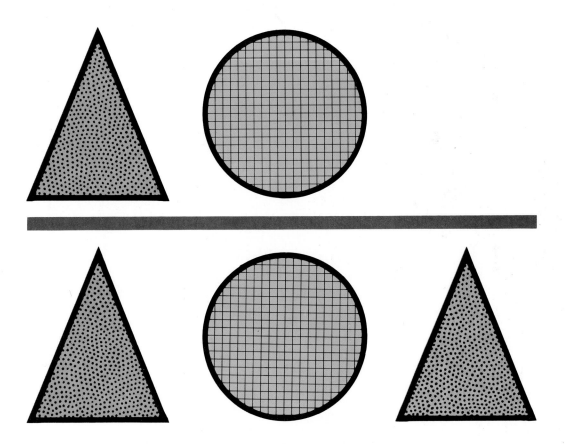

- Decide how many sections make up the form of the music.
- Point to the shapes that show the form.

  What is this form called?

Furry Bear

If I were a bear,
And a big bear too,
I shouldn't much care
If it froze or snew;
I shouldn't much mind
If it snowed or friz—
I'd be all fur-lined
With a coat like his

For I'd have fur boots and a brown fur wrap,
And brown fur knickers and a big fur cap.
I'd have a fur muffle-ruff to cover my jaws,
And brown fur mittens on my big brown paws.
With a big brown furry-down up to my head,
I'd sleep all the winter in a big fur bed.

—*A. A. Milne*

- Find the accented note (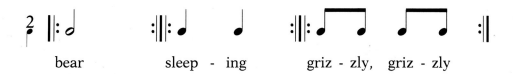) in this song.
- Practice these Bear Rhythms using the words below them.

bear   sleep - ing   griz - zly, griz - zly

- Use these words to read the rhythm of this song.

Grizzly Bear

Erling Bisgaard
Gulle Stehouwer

Griz-zly bear, a griz-zly bear is sleep-ing in a cave.

Please be ver - y qui - et, ver - y, ver - y qui - et,

If you wake him, If you shake him, he gets ver - y MAD!

ACCENT IN MUSIC

This song has many accents.

They are shown by an accent mark: >

Time to Wake Up!

Words and music by B.S.

1. Wake up I said! Time to wake up!
2. It's time to play! Time to wake up!

You sleep - y head! Time to wake up!
Out - side to stay! Time to wake up!

Get out of bed, Time to wake up!
A sun - ny day, Time to wake up!

For win - ter's past. Time to wake up!
Will come at last. Time to wake up!

Time to wake up! Time to wake up! Wake up!

ACCENT IN POETRY

To a Groundhog on February 2

Wake up, sleepyhead!
Put your dreams away.
Everyone is waiting
for what you have to say:
Will your shadow make a blot
on the snow today or not?
Will the sun start turning hot?
Will the month be cold, or what?
Hurry, sir, and tell us on this Groundhog Day.

Wake up, sleepyhead!
What's a little snow?
If your shadow follows you,
back inside you'll go.
Will the coming six weeks be
wintry, cold and shivery?
Balmy, warm, and summery?
Groundhog, what's your prophecy?
Better put your *glasses* on, so you'll really know!

—*Aileen Fisher*

● Decide which words in this poem you would
accent.

131

GRAY SQUIRREL'S SONG MAP

● Follow the path with Gray Squirrel and sing these songs.

1. "Star Light, Star Bright"

6. "The More We Get Together"

2. "Time to Wake Up!"

3. "Chicken Soup with Rice"

4. "Jim Along, Josie"

5. "Time to Wake Up!"

133

JUST CHECKING

See how much you can remember.

1. Which rhythm sounds as long as this note: ♩ ?

    a. ♩ ♩ ♩   b. ♩ ♩

2. Which rhythm sounds as long as this note: ♩. ?

    a. ♩ ♩ ♩   b. ♩ ♩

3. Point to the note that will sound louder.

    a. ♩   b. ♩
       >

4. What is the name of the sign under this note: ♩ ?
                                               >

    a.   accent   b.   decrescendo

5. Point to the note on the strong beat in each measure.

6. Look at these pitches.
   Some of them are named.
   Give the pitch syllables or scale numbers of the other pitches.

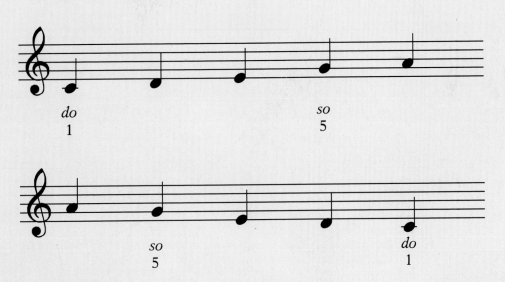

UNIT 6 SOUNDS OF SPECIAL DAYS

George Washington's Entry into New York, 1857, Currier and Ives lithograph. From the Harry T. Peters Collection, THE MUSEUM OF THE CITY OF NEW YORK.

SOUNDS OF THE ORCHESTRA

There are four instrument families in the orchestra.
How many instruments can you name in each
family?

String Family

● Listen to each instrument family.

The Young Person's Guide to the Orchestra (excerpt) by Benjamin Britten

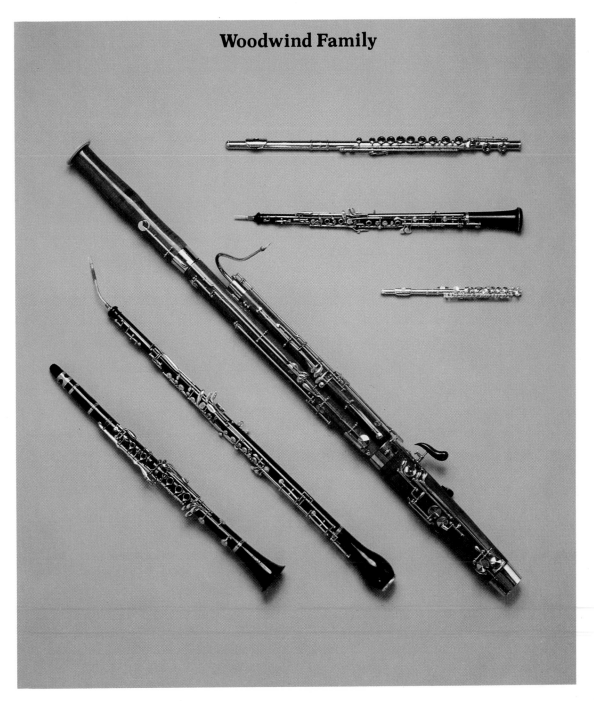

Woodwind Family

Brass Family

Percussion Family

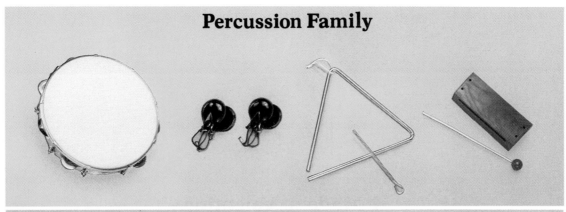

● Pat this rhythm with the song.

I Made a Valentine

Music by Lynn Freeman Olson

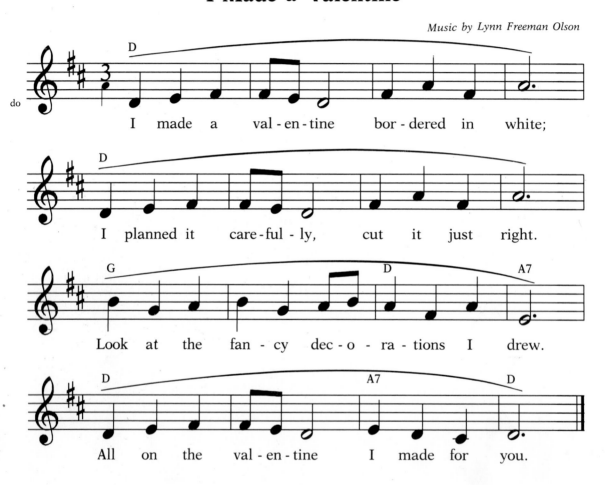

I made a val-en-tine bor-dered in white;

I planned it care-ful-ly, cut it just right.

Look at the fan-cy dec-o-ra-tions I drew.

All on the val-en-tine I made for you.

● Sing the song again.
● Play this rhythm $\frac{3}{4}$ ‖: 𝅗𝅥. :‖ on the strong
beat.

Remember 𝅗𝅥. sounds for three beats in this song.

- Put your fingers on the arrows.
- Trace the red heart with your fingers as you sing the first line of the song.
- Trace the purple heart as you sing the second line.
- Trace the lace heart as you sing the third line.
- Trace the blue heart as you sing the last line.

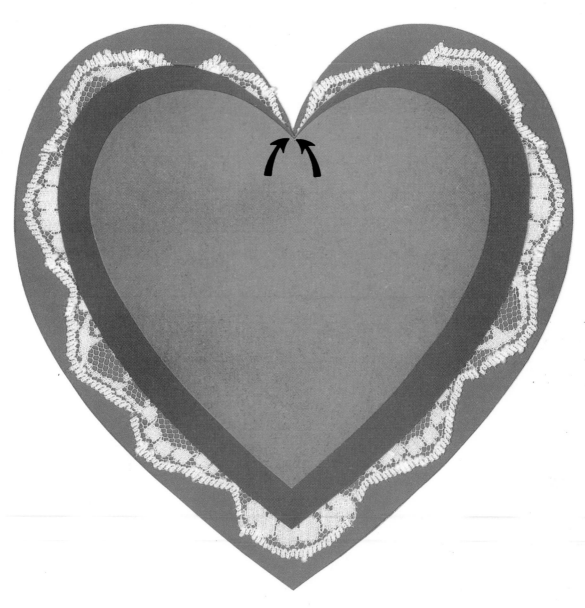

A NEW PITCH

● Find the highest note in this song.

It is called high *do* and is written as *do'*.

There's a Little Wheel A-Turnin' in My Heart

African American Folk Song

1. There's a lit-tle wheel a-turn-in' in my heart.

There's a lit-tle wheel a-turn-in' in my heart.

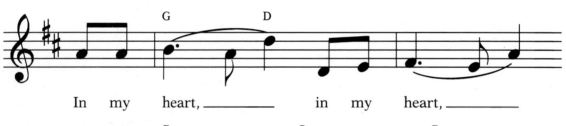

In my heart, _____ in my heart, _____

There's a lit-tle wheel a-turn-in' in my heart.

Cut-out and Applied Watercolor Love Token from New England, Private Collection, Photo © Schechter Lee

2. There's a little bell a-ringin' in my heart.

3. There's a little drum a-beatin' in my heart.

4. There's a little song a-singin' in my heart.

The hearts in this art are all cut out of paper.

What do you know about Abraham Lincoln?

Abraham Lincoln

Lincoln was a long man.
He liked out of doors.
He liked the wind blowing
And the talk in country stores.

He liked telling stories,
He liked telling jokes.
"Abe's quite a character,"
Said quite a lot of folks.

That is how they met and talked,
Knowing and unknowing.
Lincoln was the green pine.
Lincoln kept on growing.

—*Rosemary and*
Stephen Vincent Benét

VALENTINE RHYTHMS

● Clap and say these rhythms.

Each heart stands for one beat.

Sometimes two sounds are on one beat.

1. friend

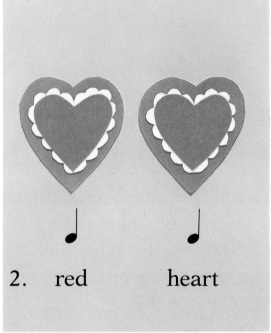

2. red　　heart

3. will you　　be my

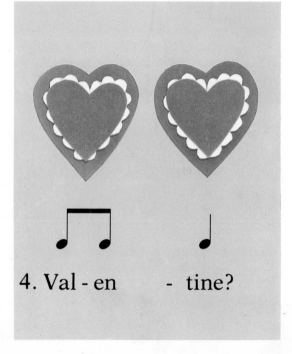

4. Val - en　　- tine?

When You Send a Valentine

*Words and music by Mildred J. Hill
and Louella Garrett*

When you send a Val - en - tine,

That's the time for fun.

Push it un - der - neath the door,

Ring the bell and run, run, run, run.

Ring the bell and run.

This song was a favorite in
Abraham Lincoln's time.

Shoo, Fly

American Folk Song

Shoo, fly, don't both - er me, Shoo, fly, don't both - er me,

Shoo, fly, don't both - er me, For I be-long to some-bo - dy.

I feel, I feel, I feel, I feel like a morn -ing star, I

feel, I feel, I feel, I feel, I feel like a morn -ing star. Oh,

Shoo, fly, don't both - er me, Shoo, fly, don't both - er me,

Shoo, fly, don't both - er me, For I be-long to some-bod - y.

● Do this dance with "Shoo, Fly."

The circle turns inside out during the B Section.

KEEP THE BEAT

We Love the U.S.A.

Music by John Philip Sousa
Words by Beatrice Krone

1. We love the U. S. A. _____
2. We love the U. S. A. _____

We live in a land where all are free,
We'll join in the chor - us loud and strong,

and proud to de - fend their li - ber - ty.
and sing of the land where we be - long.

We mean it when we say, _____

"We're glad we're a - live and live in the

U. S. A." _____

● March to the beat. Sing the song.

● As you listen, move to this march.

 "El Capitán" by John Philip Sousa

DIFFERENT TONE COLORS

● Listen to each instrument family play "Yankee Doodle."

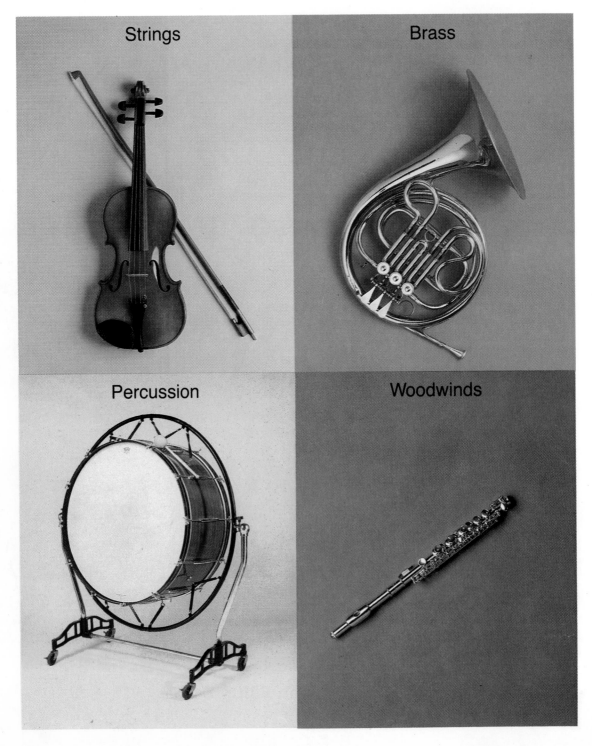

Strings

Brass

Percussion

Woodwinds

This song was a favorite in
George Washington's time.

Yankee Doodle

Traditional

Verse

1. Fath'r and   I   went down to camp A - long with Cap-tain Good-in,
2. Yan - kee Doo-dle went to town, A - rid - ing on   a   po - ny,

And there we saw the men and boys As thick as ha-sty pud-din'.
He stuck a feath-er   in   his cap And called it mac-a - ro - ni.

Refrain

Yan - kee Doo-dle keep it up,   Yan - kee Doo-dle   dan - dy.

Mind the mu - sic   and the step and   with the girls be   hand - y.

This oil painting shows
George Washington on his
horse. The artist, Thomas
Sully, is known for his
paintings of important
people.

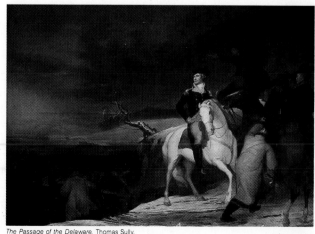

The Passage of the Delaware, Thomas Sully,
THE MUSEUM OF FINE ARTS, Boston, Massachusetts

153

● Sing this song for the Chinese New Year.

Ai Hai Yo

Shansi Melody

Ai hai yo Ai hai yo Ai hai yo hai yo.

Land of drag-ons and the sun,   the New Year has be-gun.

Go back to the beginning and sing to the End
(Da Capo al Fine)

In our homes and fields we will have a good year.

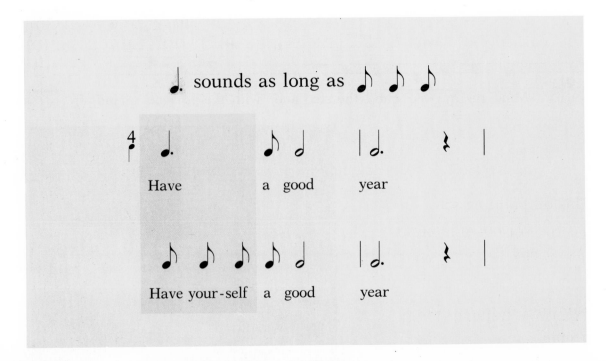

gong

temple blocks

● Find these patterns in "Ai Hai Yo."

finger cymbals

These instruments are used in some Chinese music.

Which instrument is heard with the song?

MAKE UP YOUR OWN MUSIC

- Play a steady beat using these pitches in any order you choose. Be sure to use *do'*.
- Sing "Ai Hai Yo" and play the beat.

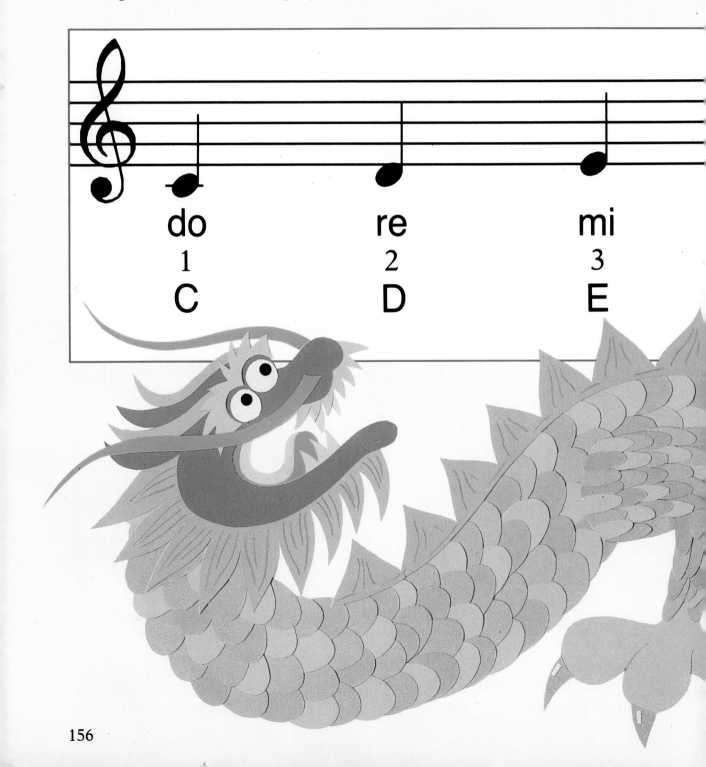

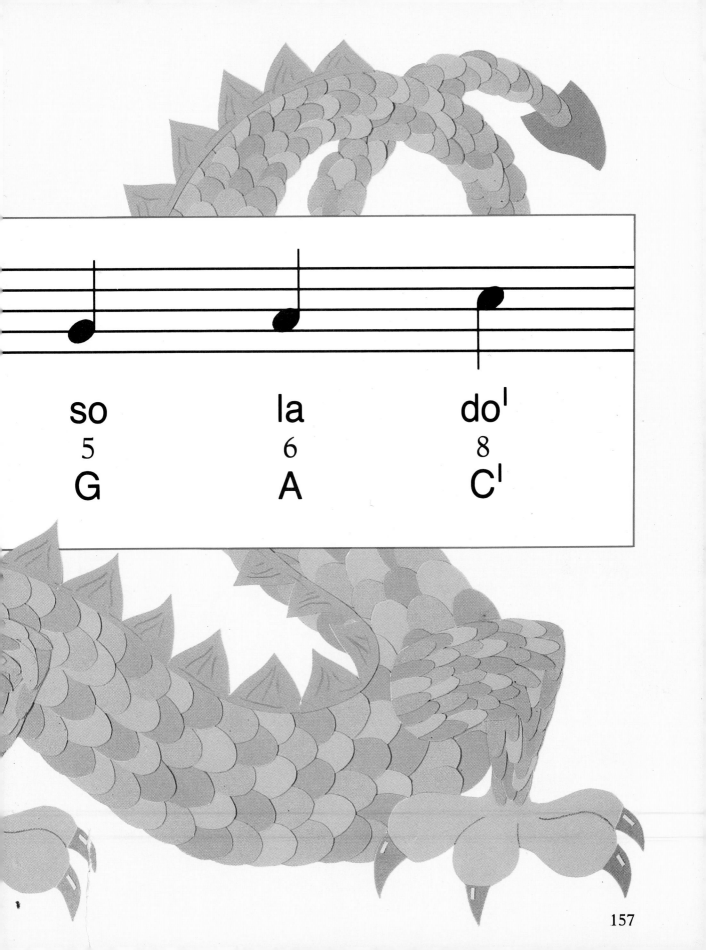

- Find the pitches *do mi so do¹* in this song.
- Find *re* and *la.*
- Sing the pitches for the song.

Old Woman and the Pig

American Folk Song

1. There was an old wom-an and she had a lit-tle pig,— Oink, oink,
2. This lit-tle old wom-an kept the pig— in the barn,— Oink, oink,

oink.   There was an old wom-an and she had a lit-tle pig,   He
oink.   This lit-tle old wom-an kept the pig— in the barn,   The

did-n't cost much 'cause he was-n't ver-y big,— Oink, oink, oink.
pret-ti-est thing she— had— on the farm,— Oink, oink, oink.

158

● Move to show *do'*.

Bluebird, Bluebird

Refrain

Blue-bird, blue-bird, through my win-dow, Blue-bird, blue-bird,

through my win-dow, Blue-bird, blue-bird, through my win-dow,

Oh, John-ny, aren't you tired? _____

Verse

Choose a lit-tle {girl boy} and tap {her him} on the shoul-der,

Choose a lit-tle {girl boy} and tap {her him} on the shoul-der,

Choose a lit-tle {girl boy} and tap {her him} on the shoul-der,

Oh, John-ny, aren't you tired? _____

159

WHO WILL LEAD THE ORCHESTRA?

string family

percussion family

woodwind family

brass family

The orchestra needs a leader.

● Choose one.

JUST CHECKING

See how much you remember.

1. Match the names of the four families of orchestral instruments with their pictures.

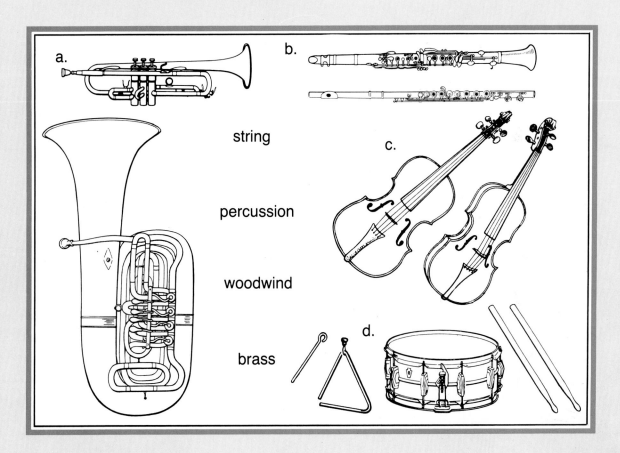

2. This note ♩ sounds as long as these two notes ♪ ♪.

   This note ♩. sounds as long as how many ♪ ?

3. a. Which note is *do*?

   b. Which note is *so*?

   c. Which note is high *do* (*do'*)?

UNIT 7 SOUNDS OF EARLY SPRING

THE BRASS FAMILY

tuba

trumpet

164

● Listen to the instruments of the brass family.

"Brass Instruments"

French horn

trombone

How are brass
instruments alike?
How are they different?

● Name the brass instrument in this song.

We Are Good Musicians

German Folk Song

Group: Oh we are good mu - si - cians and we play in the band.
Group: We'll dem - on - strate our in - stru - ments so you will un - der - stand.

Solo: I play the trum - pet. Lis - ten to the trum - pet.
Group: We play the trum - pet. Lis - ten to the trum - pets. Ta -

Solo: ta - ta - ta, Ta - ta - ta - ta, Ta - ta - ta - ta - ta - ta. Ta -
Group: ta - ta - ta, Ta - ta - ta - ta, Ta - ta - ta - ta - ta - ta.

2. I play the drum. We play the drum. Listen to the...
   Boom-boom...

3. I play the piccolo. We play the piccolo. Listen to the...
   Toot-toot...

4. Solo: Ich bin ein Musikante, und komm aus Schwabenland.
   Group: Wir sind die Musikanten, und komm'n aus Schwabenland.

   Solo: Ich kann spielen,
   Group: Wir können spielen.

   Solo: Auf der Trompete,
   Group: Auf der Trompete.

   Solo: Ta-ra-ta-ta, Ta-ra-ta-ta, Ta-ra-ta-ta-ta-ta.
   Group: Ta-ra-ta-ta, Ta-ra-ta-ta, Ta-ra-ta-ta-ta-ta.

166

MORE ABOUT THE BRASS FAMILY

This child is choosing a brass instrument.

● Listen and tap the beat.

Listen to the Brasses

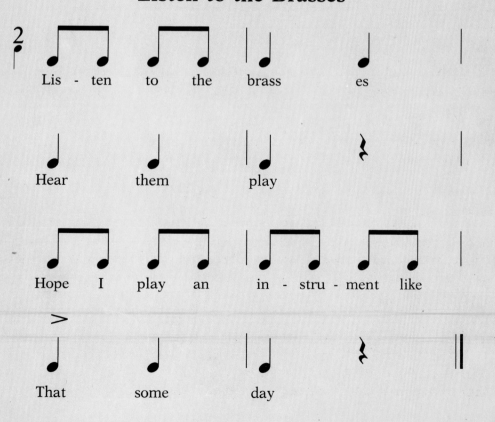

Lis - ten to the brass es

Hear them play

Hope I play an in - stru - ment like

That some day

● Listen to a royal march.

The king's children are coming to meet their new teacher.

● As the children march, listen for the brass instruments.

 "March of the Siamese Children" from *The King and I,* by Richard Rodgers

RONDO FORM

This is how the music sections go together in
"March of the Siamese Children."

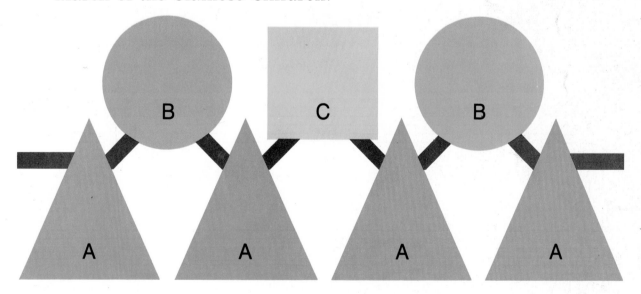

The same **melody,** or tune, is heard four times with
different melodies in between.

This form is called rondo.

● Move to show rondo form.

Rondo

Traditional Tune
Words Adapted

There is a form that we all know and
Ron - do is its name - o!
R - o - n - d - o, r - o - n - d - o,
r - o - n - d - o, and ron-do is its name - o!

- Make up a rondo with this song.
- Play this pattern four times on a classroom instrument for a B section.

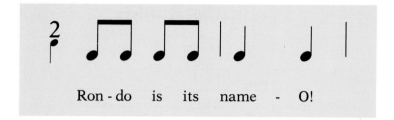

Ron - do   is   its   name - O!

- Pat or clap the pattern below four times for a C section.

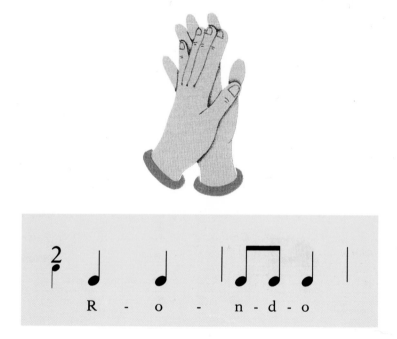

R - o - n - d - o

- Perform the rondo in this order.

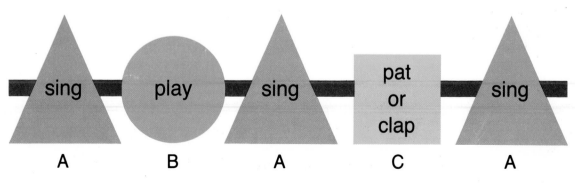

sing   play   sing   pat or clap   sing

A   B   A   C   A

LOUD AND SOFT

How many ways can you sing "Oh, yes!"?

John the Rabbit

American Folk Game Song

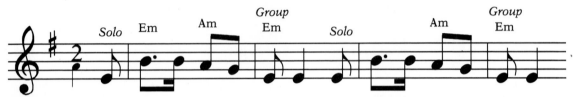

Old John the rab-bit, Oh, yes! Old John the rab-bit, Oh, yes!

Got a might-y bad hab-it, Oh, yes! Of go-ing to my gar-den, Oh, yes!

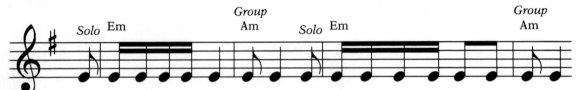

And eat-ing up my peas, Oh, yes! And cut-ting down my cab-bage, Oh, yes!

He ate to-ma-toes, Oh, yes! And sweet po-ta-toes, Oh, yes!

And if I live, Oh, yes! To see next fall, Oh, yes!

I won't plant, Oh, yes! A gar-den at all! Oh, yes!

- Pat this rhythm.
- Dance to this rhythm. Do the "Bunny Hop."

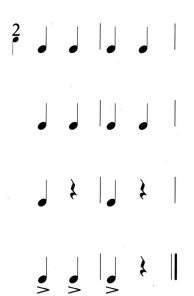

Can you tell from this picture what the rabbits are having for supper?

What movement will you do on the accented beats?

RING INTO SPRING

- Pat the strong beat while you sing this song.
- Play this rhythm $\frac{3}{2}$ ‖: 𝅗𝅥. :‖ on the strong beat. Use F and C together.

𝅗𝅥. sounds for three beats in this song.

Hear the Bells Ring

Konnie Saliba

Hear the bells ring. Ring-a-ling-a-ling-a, Ring-a-ling-a-ling-a,

Hear the bells ring. Ring-a-ling-a-ling-a, ling.

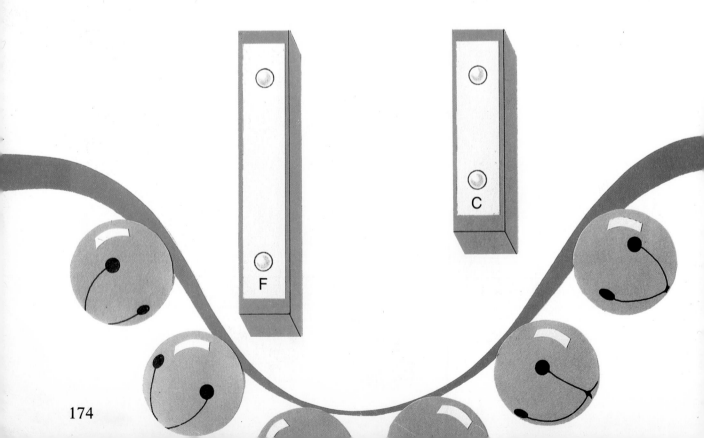

- Look at this pattern.

- Find *do*. Find the pitches that are higher than *do*. What are their names?

Ring,   Hear the bells ring - ing.

- Play the pattern on these bells.

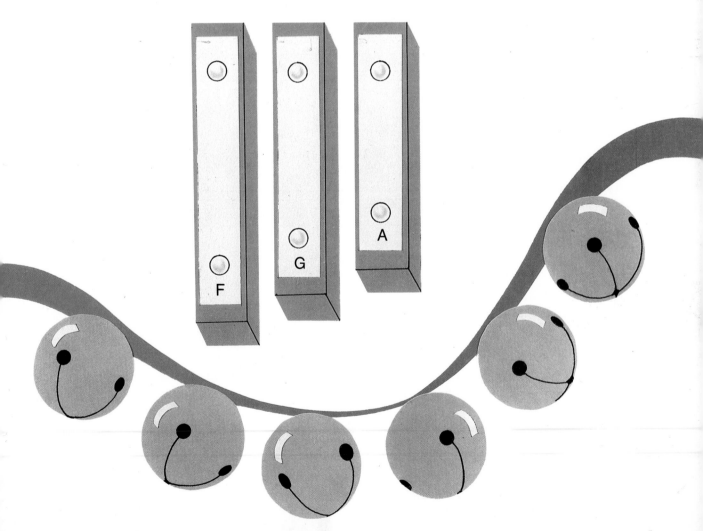

- Sing the song.
- Sing the first line, think the second line, sing the rest of the song.

Mister Rabbit

African American Play Song

Verse

1. "Mis-ter Rab-bit, Mis-ter Rab-bit, your ears might-y long!"
2. "Mis-ter Rab-bit, Mis-ter Rab-bit, your foot's might-y red!"

"Yes, in - deed, they're put on wrong."_
"Yes, in - deed, I'm al - most dead." _

Refrain

Ev - 'ry lit - tle soul must shine, shine, shine. _

Ev - 'ry lit - tle soul must shine, _ shine, shine.

3. "Your coat's mighty gray!"
   "Yes, indeed, 'twas made that way." *Refrain*

4. "Your tail's mighty white!"
   "Yes, indeed, I'm going out of sight." *Refrain*

176

● Listen to these songs about rabbits.

"Bunny Hop" is the A section.

"Mister Rabbit" is the B section.

"John the Rabbit" is the C section.

This is how the sections go together to make a
"Rabbit Rondo."

A B A C A

A RONDO OF CLOCKS

● Listen to "The Viennese Musical Clock."

 "The Viennese Musical Clock" from *Háry János Suite,* by Zoltán Kodály

How do these pictures go with the music?

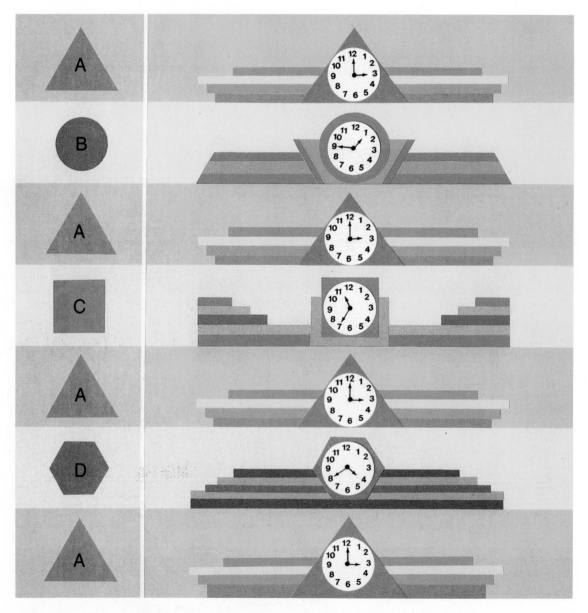

"The Viennese Musical Clock" is in rondo form because the first section returns after each different section.

- Sing the clock melody you heard in "Viennese Musical Clock."

List - en to the clock, let's list - en to the clock.

- Play the clock melody using these pitches.

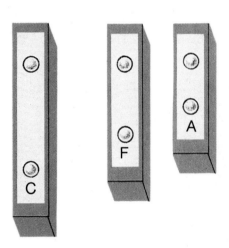

This is one of the many clocks in the city of Munich.

HEARING *so,* *do* AND *mi*

Y'a un Rat

Traditional

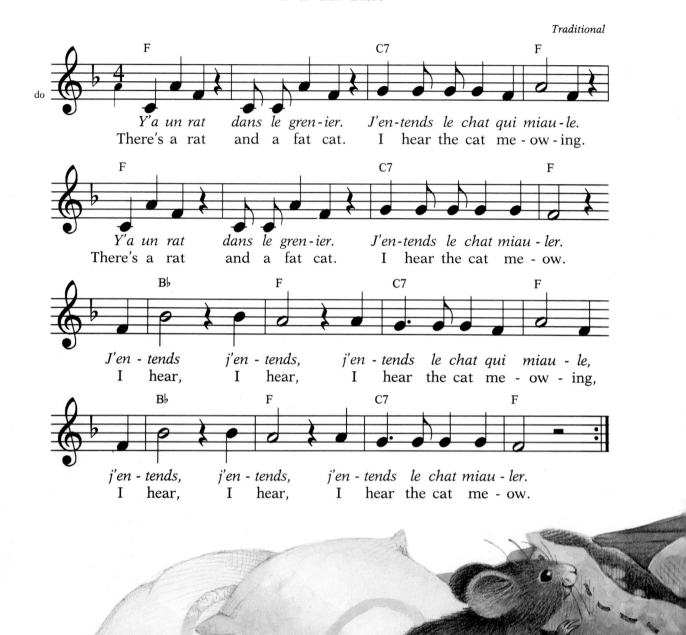

Y'a un rat dans le gren-ier. J'en-tends le chat qui miau-le.
There's a rat and a fat cat. I hear the cat me-ow-ing.

Y'a un rat dans le gren-ier. J'en-tends le chat miau-ler.
There's a rat and a fat cat. I hear the cat me-ow.

J'en-tends j'en-tends, j'en-tends le chat qui miau-le,
I hear, I hear, I hear the cat me-ow-ing,

j'en-tends, j'en-tends, j'en-tends le chat miau-ler.
I hear, I hear, I hear the cat me-ow.

● Listen for pitches you know.

When do you hear *so₁ mi do* in "Y'a un Rat"?
         5₁ 3 1

SPRING WINDS

Can you see the wind?
How can you tell that the wind
is blowing?

Who Has Seen the Wind?

Who has seen the wind?
　Neither I nor you:
But when the leaves hang trembling,
　The wind is passing through.

Who has seen the wind?
　Neither you nor I:
But when the trees bow down their heads,
　The wind is passing by.

　　　　　　　　　—Christina Rossetti

Let's Go Fly a Kite

Music by Richard M. Sherman
Words by Robert B. Sherman

Verse

1. With __ tup-pence for pa-per and strings, ___
2. When you send __ it fly-ing up there, ___

You can have your own set of wings; ___
All at once you're light-er than air; ___

With your feet on the ground you're a bird in flight
You can dance on the breeze o-ver hous-es and trees

With your fist hold - ing tight ___
With your fist hold - ing tight ___

to the string of your kite. Oh! ___
to the string of your kite. Oh! ___

184

Refrain

Let's go fly a kite, Up to the high-est height!

Let's go fly a kite, And send it soar-ing,

Up through the at-mos-phere, Up where the air is clear.

Oh, let's go ___ fly a kite! ___

● Find this pattern in "Let's Go Fly a Kite."

● Point to each note as you sing it.

A RHYTHM PATTERN
TO SAY AND CLAP

Sometimes you see eighth notes with beams:

Sometimes you see eighth notes with flags:

● Find two kinds of eighth notes in this music.

There was an old man named Mi - chael Fin - ni - gin.

● Find the eighth notes in this pattern.

Don't quit, be - gin a - gain

Poor old Mi - chael

● Say the pattern.

A NEW FORM

Michael Finnigin

American Folk Song

1. There was an old man named Mi - chael Fin - ni - gin.

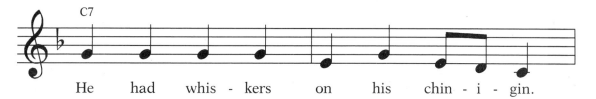

He had whis - kers on his chin - i - gin.

Wind blew them off but they grew in a - gain.

Poor old Mi - chael Fin - ni - gin! Be - gin a - gain!

2. There was an old man named Michael Finnigin.
   Built a house of sticks and tin again.
   Wind came along and blew it in again.
   Poor old Michael Finnigin! Begin again!

3. There was an old man named Michael Finnigin.
   Went out fishing with a pin again.
   Caught a_whale that jumped back in again.
   Poor old Michael Finnigin! Begin again!

SING SOME SONGS FOR SPRING

● Put together songs you know to make a rondo.

Sing "Rondo" as the A part.

Sing other songs as the B and C parts.

The different shapes show how the parts go together.

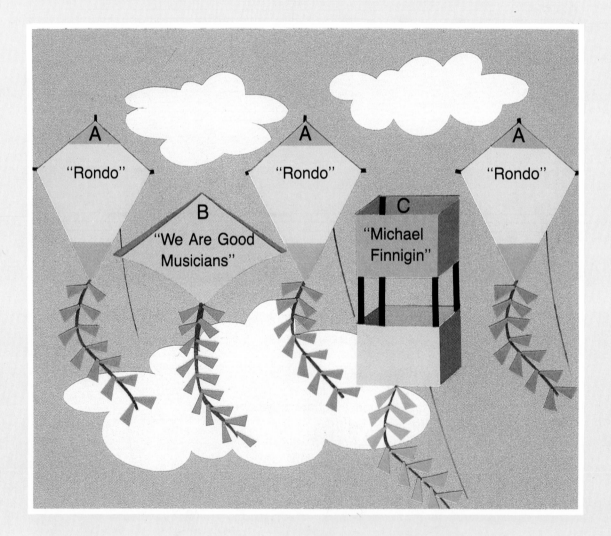

● Listen for the sound of the trumpet in "We Are
Good Musicians."

188

JUST CHECKING

See how much you remember.

1. Look at these pictures of four brass instruments.

   Which name is missing?

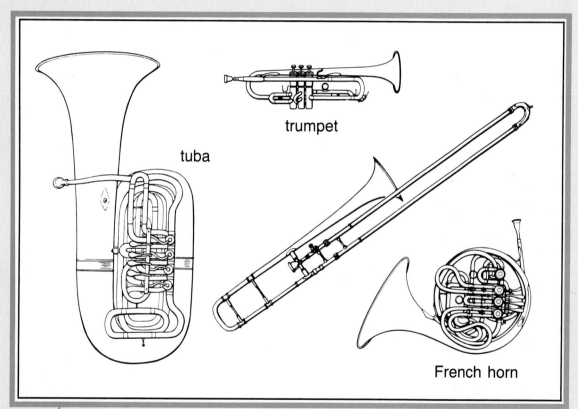

2. Point to the smallest brass instrument.

3. Which letters show rondo form?

   A B A   A B A C A   A B

4. Point to the notes that are the same as

UNIT 8 CONTRASTS IN MUSIC

CONTRASTS

If Things Grew Down

If things grew down
Instead of up,
A dog would grow
Into a pup.
A cat would grow
Into a kitten.
Your sweater would grow
Into a mitten.
A cow would grow
Into a calf.
And a whole would grow
Into a half.
Big would grow
Into something small
And small would grow
Into nothing at all.

—*Robert D. Hoeft*

Contrasts show differences.

● Find a contrast in "If Things Grew Down."

Music has contrasts, too.

● Match the contrasts.

faster	softer
higher	shorter
louder	lower
longer	slower

● Listen for contrasts.

"Contrasts in Music"

"Bourrée" from *Music for the Royal Fireworks*
by George Frederick Handel

193

● Find the contrasts in the words.

High Is Better Than Low

*Words and Music by Howard Dietz
and Arthur Schwartz*

High is bet-ter than low, Joy is bet-ter than woe,

Glad is bet-ter than sad, And just in case you did-n't know,

Up is bet-ter than down, Smile is bet-ter than frown;

Don't be drag-ging a fear-ful, tear-ful face a-round the town.

If your spir-it is bub-bly you'll win man-y a friend,

Bub-bly's bet-ter than trou-bly, so I rec-om-mend ―

194

Sing wher-ev-er you go, High is bet-ter than low,

You'll be bet-ter if you say it's so. _____

LONGER SOUNDS, SHORTER SOUNDS

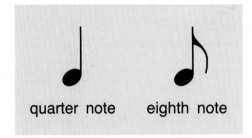

quarter note   eighth note

Which of these notes stands for a longer sound?

Which of these notes stands for a shorter sound?

● Say these rhythms.

walk   walk   walk   walk

Quarter notes can sound like walking steps.

jog-ging jog-ging jog-ging jog-ging

Eighth notes can sound like jogging steps.

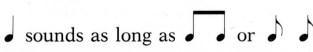

- Pat eighth notes during the A section.
- Step quarter notes on the beat during the B section.

Run, Children, Run

Translation and words adapted by
Millie Burnett

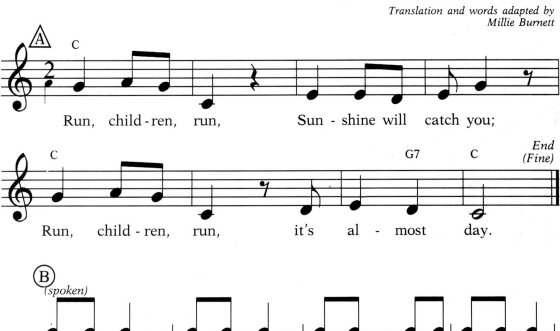

Run, child-ren, run, Sun-shine will catch you;

Run, child-ren, run, it's al-most day.

(spoken)

That child ran, that child flew, that child lost his Sun-day shoe.

Go back to the beginning and sing to the end.
(Da Capo al Fine)

Tell you what I'm going to do. I'm going to find his Sun-day shoe.

BEAT AND STRONG BEAT
Tromm, Tromm, Tromm

English Adaptation by
Doreen Hall and Arnold Walter

Tromm,   tromm,   tromm,

Come see my   new red   drum.

It's real-ly   lots of   fun

To march in   time and   sing in   rhyme and

Beat up - on my   drum,   trrromm!

trrromm!

trrromm!

Which drums in each row show the strong beat?

This is one way to show beat.

This is another way to show beat. It also shows beats in sets of two.

If beats are in sets of two, the first beat is usually the strong beat.

Which way sounds like you are walking with one shoe off?

● Play this pattern. Make the strong beats a little louder than the other beats.

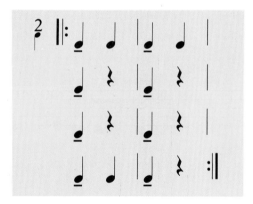

● Play the same pattern with "Walking Song."

 "Walking Song" from *Acadian Songs and Dances* by Virgil Thomson

CONTRASTS BETWEEN
SOFT AND LOUD

Another word for soft is **piano (*p*).** Another word for
loud is **forte (*f*).**

Who's That Tapping at the Window?

Traditional

Who's that tap - ping at the win - dow?

Who's that knock - ing at the door?

I am tap - ping at the win - dow.

I am knock - ing at the door.

- Follow the music symbols as you listen to this music.

 "Parade" from *Divertissement* by Jacques Ibert

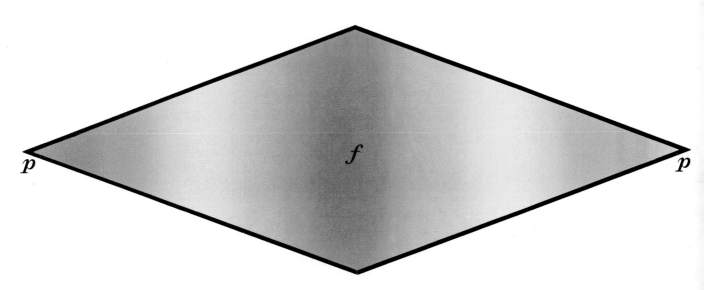

p   *f*   *p*

Here comes the parade.   There goes the parade.

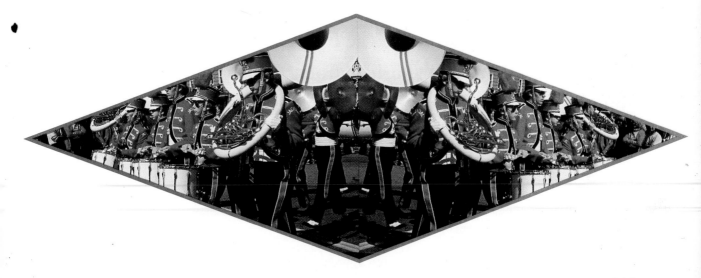

UPWARD AND DOWNWARD

Some parts of this bridge are very high.

upward

downward

Brooklyn Bridge, Variations on an Old Theme, Joseph Stella,
Collection of the WHITNEY MUSEUM OF AMERICAN ART, NY

Some parts of this bridge are very low.

- Look at the bridge from low to high.
- Look at the bridge from high to low.
- Move your arms to show upward and downward in this music.

 "Fountain Dance" from *Wand of Youth Suite No. 2* by Edward Elgar

Do the first three notes in each line of this song
move upward or downward?

Long-Legged Sailor

Game Chant

1. Did you ev - er, ev - er, ev - er in your long - leg-ged life

Meet a long - leg-ged sail - or with a long - leg-ged wife?

No I nev - er, nev - er, nev - er in my long - leg-ged life

Met a long - leg-ged sail - or with a long - leg-ged wife.

2. short-legged   3. knock-kneed   4. bow-legged   5. cross-legged

The sign ⌢ over a note means that you hold the
note a little longer.

CONTRASTS IN TEXTURE

Cloth has texture.

How are the textures the same?

How are the textures different?

Music has texture, too.

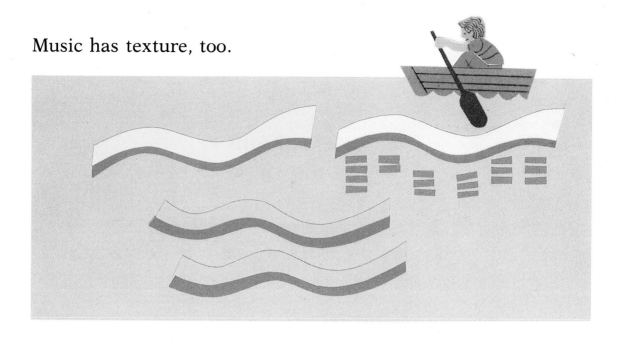

Row, Row, Row Your Boat

Traditional Round

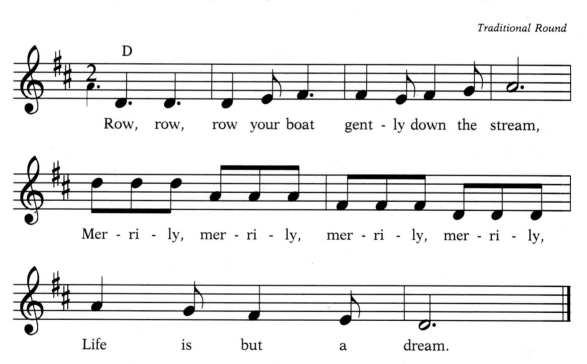

Row, row, row your boat gent - ly down the stream,

Mer - ri - ly, mer - ri - ly, mer - ri - ly, mer - ri - ly,

Life is but a dream.

● Listen to "Row, Row, Row Your Boat" played

three ways.

Each way has a different musical texture.

SAME AND DIFFERENT

● Use your speaking voice when you see notes that look like this:

One Day My Mother
Went to the Market

Italian Folk Tune
Words by Leo Israel

Verse

1. One day my moth - er went to the mar - ket

And she bought a hand - some roost - er.

A roost - er? A roost - er!

But when my moth - er start - ed to cook him,

He did ev' - ry - thing he use - ta.

He use - ta? He use - ta!

Refrain

Oh, he said, "Cock - a - doo - dle - doo,

How I love you, how I love you."

Oh, he said, "Cock - a - doo - dle - doo."

And a - way he flew, and a - way he flew.

2. . . .and she bought a little pig. . .
But when my mother started to cook him,
He got up and danced a jig. . .
Oh, he said, "Oink, oink, oink,
Though I'd like to stay, though I'd like to stay."
Oh, he said, "Oink, oink, oink,"
And he ran away, and he ran away.

3. . . .and she bought a pretty lamb. . .
But when my mother started to cook him,
He said, "Who do you think I am?". . .
Oh, he said, "Baa, baa, baa,
I'm silly, it's true, I'm silly, it's true."
Oh, he said, "Baa, baa, baa,
Not as silly as you, not as silly as you."

4. . . . and she bought a lovely hen . . .
But when my mother started to cook her,
She began to cluck again . . .
Oh, she said, "Cluck, cluck, cluck, cluck, cluck."
But she forgot, but she forgot,
Oh, she said, "Cluck, cluck, cluck, cluck, cluck,"
And fell into the pot, and fell into the pot.

207

- Listen to "Bourrée" by Handel for sections that are the same. Are some sections different?

- Show the form as you move to the music like sparklers, spinners, and rockets.

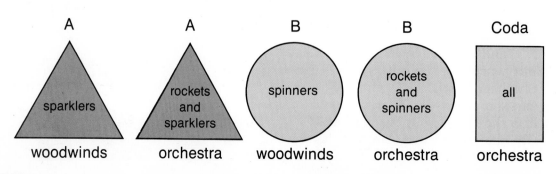

A	A	B	B	Coda
sparklers	rockets and sparklers	spinners	rockets and spinners	all
woodwinds	orchestra	woodwinds	orchestra	orchestra

- Find the pictures that are the same.
- Find the pictures that are different.

What form does this picture show?

A

B

A

C

A

- Listen for the sections in this rondo.

"Walking Song" (complete) from *Acadian Songs and Dances* by Virgil Thomson

CONTRASTS IN TONE COLOR

Every instrument has its own special sound—its
own **tone color.**

● Listen again to "Bourrée" by Handel. Point to the
picture that shows what you are hearing. Once
you hear when the timpani plays, can you guess
when it will play again?

● Name the instruments you hear in each verse.

Going over the Sea

Canadian Street Rhyme

1. When I was one I ate a bun, Go-ing o-ver the sea. I

jumped a-board a sail-or-man's ship, And the sail-or-man said to me,

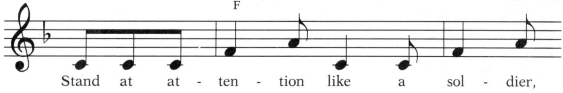

"Go - ing o - ver, go - ing un - der,

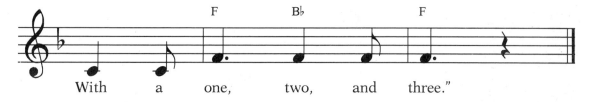

Stand at at - ten - tion like a sol - dier,

With a one, two, and three."

2. When I was two I buckled my shoe,

3. When I was three I banged my knee,

4. When I was four I shut the door,

5. When I was five I learned to jive,

6. When I was six I picked up sticks,

7. When I was seven I went to heaven,

8. When I was eight I learned to skate,

9. When I was nine I climbed a vine,

10. When I was ten I caught a hen,

CONTRASTS IN RHYTHMS

This jogging rhythm has short sounds.

short   short   short   short
jog——ging   jog——ging

This galloping rhythm has both long

and short sounds.

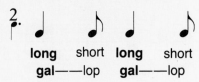

long   short   long   short
gal——lop   gal——lop

Which rhythm goes with this song?

Matarile

Mexican Folk Song

1. ¿Qué quiere us - ted? Ma - ta - ri - le, ri - le, ri - le.
   Quie - ro sal - tar, Ma - ta - ri - le, ri - le, ri - le.

¿Qué quiere us - ted? Ma - ta - ri - le, ri - le, ron.
Quie - ro sal - tar, Ma - ta - ri - le, ri - le, ron.

2. *What do you want? Matarile, rile, rile.*
   What do you want? Matarile, rile, ron.

   I want to jump, Matarile, rile, rile.
   I want to jump, Matarile, rile, ron.

● Add other verses using the words *Quiero marchar*

   (I want to march) and *Quiero correr (I want to run).*

NAMING RHYTHMS

Which rhythm goes with this song?

Pop Goes the Weasel

American Singing Game

A pen-ny for a spool_of thread, A pen-ny for a nee-dle.

That's the way the mon-ey goes, Pop! goes the wea-sel.

SING AND MOVE

Can you name songs that go with these pictures?

What contrasts are in these songs?

JUST CHECKING

See how much you remember.

1. Which pair does not show a contrast?

   a.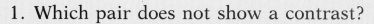

   b. upward/downward

   c. longer/shorter

   d. louder/softer

2. Which note sounds longer?

   a. 𝅘𝅥

   b. 𝅘𝅥𝅮

3. Point to an eighth note on this page.

4. Point to a quarter note on this page.

5. How many parts will sound the same in this form?

   △A ◯B △A ▢C △A

6. Which note pattern shows a gallop rhythm?

   a. ♫ ♩ ♫ ♩   b. ♩ ♪ ♩ ♪

LOOKING BACK OVER THE YEAR

"Bingo"

"False Face"

"Michael Finnigin"

● Look through this book and remember your favorite songs.

216

"Clickety Clack"

"Jingle Bells"

"Chicken Soup with Rice"

"There's a Little Wheel A-Turnin'"

"Going Over the Sea"

● Tell one thing you learned about music from a favorite song.

THE BREMEN TOWN MUSICIANS

Words and music by John Horman

Act One

Once there was an old donkey who had worked hard all his life. When his master didn't want him any more he decided to run away to Bremen. As he walked along he was joined by a dog, a cat, and a rooster. This is the song they sang.

I May Be Old

The Animals
Verse *(Donkey)*

1. I may be old, or so I'm told, But I can still do ma-ny things. _

My back's not strong, the road's too long, But with my voice I love to sing. _

Refrain *f*

I am going to Bre-men Town Won't let life ___ get me down. ___

218

2. (Dog)
   I may be old, or so I'm told,
   But I can still do many things.
   My bark is weak, my tail keeps beat,
   And with my voice I'll try to sing!
   (Refrain)

3. (Cat)
   I may be old, or so I'm told,
   But I can still do many things.
   I won't catch mice, they seem so nice,
   But with my voice I love to sing!
   (Refrain)

4. (Rooster)
   I may be old, or so I'm told,
   But I can still do many things.
   I crow too loud! Because I'm proud,
   But with my voice I love to sing!
   (Refrain)

5. (All)
   We may be old, or so we're told,
   But we can still do many things.
   Good friends are we, as you can see.
   Fine music's what we now will bring.
   On our way to Bremen Town,
   Won't let life get us down.

219

The donkey, the dog, the cat, and the rooster walked all day. When night began to fall, they came to a house in the woods. They all looked in the window, and this is what they saw.

Three Men Sittin' at a Table

The Animals
Donkey ***p***

1. Three men sit-tin' at a ta-ble, three men sit-tin' at a ta-ble,

Three men sit-tin' at a ta-ble, and they look like rob-bers.

2. **(Dog)**
Food, food sittin' on the table,
Food, food sittin' on the table,
Food, food sittin' on the table,
Lookin' oh so tasty!

3. **(Cat)**
We are very, very hungry,
We are very, very hungry,
We are very, very hungry,
Wish that we could have some.

4. **(Rooster)**
If we sing our song now,
If we sing our song now,
If we sing our song now,
How could they refuse us?

The donkey had an idea. If they all sang for the robbers, the robbers would be pleased with their music and invite them to share the food. The dog stood on the donkey, the cat stood on the dog, and the rooster stood on the cat. They all began to sing.

Sing for Our Supper

The Animals

Sing! Sing! Sing for our sup - per!

Sing! Sing! Sing our sweet song.

They took turns singing their best sounds.

Hee Haw

Donkey   *Rooster*   *Cat*

Hee haw! Hee haw! Cock - a - doo - dle - doo! Me - ow!

Donkey   *Dog*

Hee haw! Hee haw! Bow wow wow wow!

Then they sang the two songs at the same time.

The animals sang so loud that they broke the window. The noise frightened the robbers and they ran from the house. The four "musicians" sang and danced as they went inside to eat.

Sit Down, Let's Eat

The Animals　　　　　　　　　　　　　(Tambourine)

The rob-bers all have run a-way!

This sure-ly is our luck-y day!

Our ser-e-nade is now com-plete!

The food is here, sit down, Let's eat!

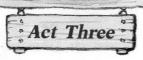

Later that night the robbers came back. The house was dark, and one of the robbers went inside to look around.

A Robber Must Be Brave

f *First Robber*

1. A rob-ber must be brave. A rob-ber must be brave.
2. A rob-ber must be brave. A rob-ber must be brave.
3. A rob-ber must be brave. A rob-ber must be brave.

First time: First Robber
Second time: Chorus

He must be bold, he must stand tall.
He must not scream, he must not shout.
He must not run, he must not hide.

First time: First Robber
Second time: Chorus

And ne-ver e-ver fear at all!
When sca-ry mon-sters roam a-bout!
Or when it thun-ders stay in-side!

Coda *First Robber*

A rob-ber must be brave! A rob-ber must be brave!

Animals   *Robbers*

Boo!   Aaaa!

What a noise! Each animal made a loud sound and chased the robber from the house. The robber ran for his life, screaming "Giants! Giants!"

Giants! Giants!

First Robber

1. They kick, they scream, they bite! And what an aw-ful sight!
2. Their eyes were fi - ery red! They bit me in the leg!

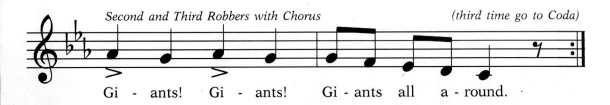

Second and Third Robbers with Chorus   *(third time go to Coda)*

Gi - ants! Gi - ants! Gi - ants all a - round.

Coda

Second and Third Robbers with Chorus

Gi - ants! Gi - ants! Gi - ants all a - round!

3. I won't go back inside! I want to stay alive!
   Giants! Giants! Giants all around.

When the other robbers heard the story they all went away, and were never seen around there again. The four "musicians" liked their new house so much that they never went to Bremen.

Home, Sweet Home

The Animals

We may be old or so we're told, But we can still do ma-ny things! _

Four friends are we, each one plus three, We help each oth-er as we sing. _

Refrain

(triangle)

We no far-ther now will roam. Four good friends, __ home sweet home. __

This art shows the four animals in the play.
Where would you see this piece of art?
What was used to make it?

SONGBOOK

Lemonade

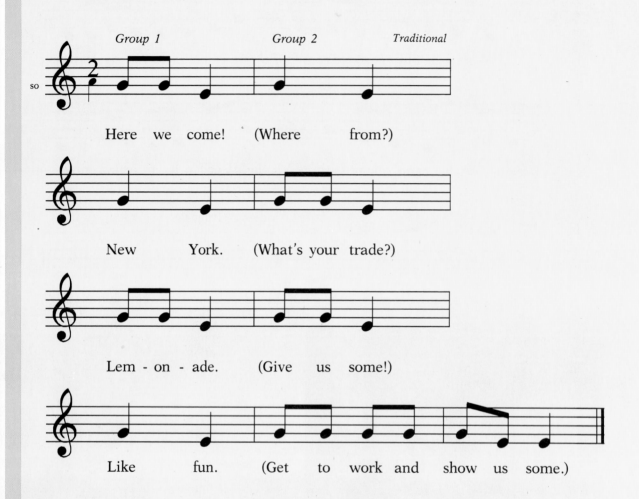

Group 1   *Group 2*   *Traditional*

Here we come! (Where from?)

New York. (What's your trade?)

Lem - on - ade. (Give us some!)

Like fun. (Get to work and show us some.)

Tinker, Tailor

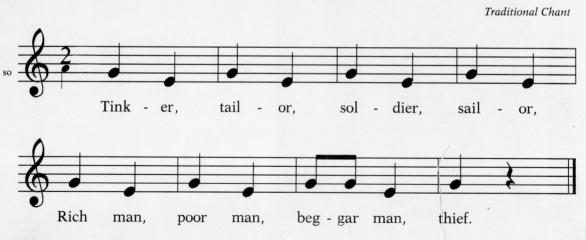

Traditional Chant

Tink - er, tail - or, sol - dier, sail - or,

Rich man, poor man, beg - gar man, thief.

We Are Playing in the Forest

Traditional

so

We are play-ing in the for-est   for the wolf is far a-way.

Who knows what will hap-pen to us   if he finds us at our play?

Lucy Locket

Traditional

so

Lu-cy Lock-et   lost her pock-et. Kit-ty Fish-er found it.

Not a pen-ny was there in it. On-ly rib-bon round it.

● Name this tune.

Mystery Tune

Traditional

do

Mouse Mousie

Hungarian Folk Song

do

Mouse Mou-sie, lit-tle mou-sie, hur-ry, hur-ry do!

Or the kit-ty in the hou-sie will be cha-sing you!
(RUN!)

Hop, Old Squirrel

American Folk Song

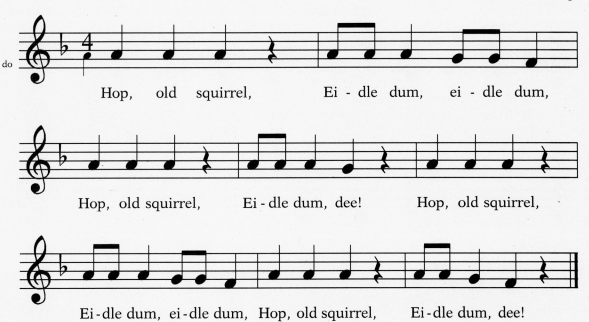

Hop, old squirrel, Ei - dle dum, ei - dle dum,

Hop, old squirrel, Ei - dle dum, dee! Hop, old squirrel,

Ei - dle dum, ei - dle dum, Hop, old squirrel, Ei - dle dum, dee!

Good News

African American Spiritual

Good news! (clap clap) Char - i - ot's com - in', Good

news! (clap clap) Char - i - ot's com - in', Good news! (clap clap)

Char - i - ot's com - in' and I don't want it to leave me be - hind.

Rover

Traditional English Rhyme
Music by Denise Bacon

1. I have a dog and his name is Ro - ver.
2. When he is good he is good all o - ver.

He is the one I love the best.
When he is bad he is just a pest.

Rocky Mountain

Southern Folk Song

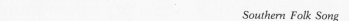

Rock - y Moun - tain, Rock - y Moun - tain, Rock - y Moun - tain high,

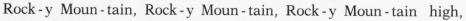

When you're on that Rock - y Moun - tain, Hang your head and cry.

Do, do, do, do, Do re - mem - ber me.

Do, do, do, do, Do re - mem - ber me.

Button, You Must Wander

Traditional

But - ton, you must wan - der, wan - der, wan - der,

But - ton, you must wan - der ev - 'ry - where.

Little Tommy Tinker

Traditional

Lit - tle Tom - my Tink - er sat up - on a clink - er And

he be - gan to cry, "Ma! ___ Ma!" ___

Poor lit - tle in - no - cent guy.

Battle Hymn of the Republic

Music by William Steffe
Words by Julia Ward Howe

Glo - ry, glo - ry, hal - le - lu - jah!

Glo - ry, glo - ry, hal - le - lu - jah!

Glo - ry, glo - ry, hal - le - lu - jah!

His truth is march - ing on.

America, the Beautiful

Music by Samuel A. Ward
Words by Katharine Lee Bates

1. O beau-ti-ful for spa-cious skies, For am-ber waves of grain,
2. O beau-ti-ful for pa-triot dream That sees be-yond the years

For pur-ple moun-tain maj-es-ties A-bove the fruit-ed plain!
Thine al-a-bas-ter cit-ies gleam, Un-dimmed by hu-man tears!

A-mer-i-ca! A-mer-i-ca! God shed His grace on thee

And crown thy good with broth-er-hood From sea to shin-ing sea!

233

There Are Many Flags in Many Lands

Composer Unknown
Words by M.H. Howliston

There are man-y flags in man-y lands, There are flags of ev-'ry hue;

But there is no flag, how-ev-er grand, Like our own Red, White _ and _ Blue.

Refrain

Then hur-rah for the flag, Our coun-try's flag, Its stripes and white stars, too;

For there is no flag in an - y land, Like our own Red, White _ and _ Blue.

Peter Cottontail

Words and music by Steve Nelson
and Jack Rollins

Here comes Peter Cottontail,
Hoppin' down the bunny trail,
Hippity hoppin', Easter's on its way.

Bringing every girl and boy
baskets full of Easter joy,
Things to make your Easter bright and gay.

He's got jelly beans for Tommy,
Colored eggs for sister Sue,
There's an orchid for your Mommy
And an Easter bonnet too,

Oh! Here comes Peter Cottontail,
Hoppin' down the bunny trail,
Hippity hoppity, Happy Easter day.

One Dark Night

Words and Music by
Lynn Freeman Olson

One dark night leaves be-gin to fly,

One black cat looks me in the eye,

One big jack-o-lan-tern grins at me, So I

know what night it is! BOO!

Must Be Santa

Words and Music
by Hal Moore and
Bill Fredricks

1.Who's got a beard that's long and white?

San-ta's got a beard that's long and white!

Who comes a-round on a spe-cial night?

San-ta comes a-round on a spe-cial night!

No repeat 1st time, repeat once more for each verse. **Refrain**

Spe-cial night, beard that's white, Must be San-ta, must be

San-ta Must be San-ta, San-ta Claus.

2. Who's got boots and a suit of red?
Santa's got. . .
Who wears a long cap on his head?
Santa wears. . .
Cap on head, suit that's red,
Special night, beard that's white,
Refrain

3. Who's got a great big cherry nose?
Santa's got. . .
Who laughs this way, "Ho, ho, ho?"
Santa laughs. . .
Ho, ho, ho, cherry nose,
Cap on head, suit that's red,
Special night, beard that's white,
Refrain

4. Who very soon will come our way?
Santa very. . .
Eight little reindeer pull his sleigh,
Santa's little. . .
Reindeer sleigh, come our way,
Ho, ho, ho, cherry nose,
Cap on head, suit that's red,
Special night, beard that's white,
Refrain

5. Dasher, Dancer, Prancer, Vixen,
Comet, Cupid, Donner, Blitzen.
Dasher, Dancer, Prancer, Vixen,
Comet, Cupid, Donner, Blitzen.
Reindeer sleigh, come our way,
Ho, ho, ho, cherry nose,
Cap on head, suit that's red,
Special night, beard that's white,
Refrain twice

"MUST BE SANTA"
Words and Music by Hal Moore and Bill Fredricks
TRO-© 1960 Hollis Music, Inc., New York, N.Y. Used by Permission

Frosty the Snow Man

Words and music by
Steve Nelson and Jack Rollins

1. Frosty the snow man was a jolly happy soul,
   With a corn cob pipe and a button nose
   and two eyes made out of coal.

   Frosty the snow man is a fairy tale, they say,
   He was made of snow but the children know
   how he came to life one day.
   There must have been some magic in that old silk hat they found.
   For when they placed it on his head he began to dance around.
   Oh, Frosty the snow man was alive as he could be,
   and the children say he could laugh and play
   just the same as you and me.

2. Frosty the snow man knew the sun was hot that day,
   So he said "Let's run and we'll have some fun
   now before I melt away."
   Down to the village, with a broomstick in his hand,
   Running here and there all around the square
   sayin', "Catch me if you can."
   He led them down the streets of town right to the traffic cop.
   And he only paused a moment when he heard him holler "stop!"
   For Frosty the snow man had to hurry on his way
   But he waved good-bye sayin' "Don't you cry,
   I'll be back again some day."

   Thumpety thump thump, thumpety thump thump,
   Look at Frosty go.
   Thumpety thump thump, thumpety thump thump,
   Over the hills of snow.

Up on the Housetop

Words and music by
Benjamin T. Hanby

1. Up on the house-top the rein-deer pause, Out jumps good old San-ta Claus;

Down through the chim - ney with lots of toys,

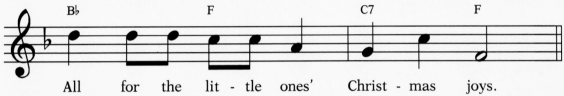

All for the lit - tle ones' Christ - mas joys.

Refrain

Ho, ho, ho, Who would-n't go! Ho, ho, ho, Who would-n't go! _

Up on the house - top, click, click, click,

Down through the chim - ney with good Saint Nick.

2.
First comes the stocking of little Nell;
Oh, dear Santa, fill it well.
Give her a dolly that laughs and cries,
One that can open and shut its eyes.
Refrain

3.
Look in the stocking of little Bill;
Oh, just see what a glorious fill!
Here is a hammer, and lots of tacks,
Whistle and a ball and a whip that cracks.
Refrain

Rudolph, the Red-Nosed Reindeer

Words and music by
Johnny Marks

You know Dasher and Dancer, and Prancer and Vixen,
Comet and Cupid and Donner and Blitzen,
but do you recall the most famous reindeer of all?

Rudolph, the red-nosed reindeer had a very shiny nose
And if you ever saw it, you would even say it glows.
All of the other reindeer used to laugh and call him names.
They never let poor Rudolph join in any reindeer games.

Then one foggy Christmas Eve, Santa came to say,
"Rudolph, with your nose so bright, won't you guide my sleigh tonight?"
Then how the reindeer loved him as they shouted out with glee:
"Rudolph the red-nosed reindeer, you'll go down in history."

Mary Had a Baby

Spiritual

1. Ma-ry had a ba-by, Yes, Lord,
Ma-ry had a ba-by, Yes, my Lord,
Ma-ry had a ba-by, Yes, Lord,
The peo-ple keep a-com-ing and the train has gone.

2. What did Mary name him. . .

3. Mary named him Jesus. . .

4. Where was Jesus born. . .

5. Born in lowly stable. . .

6. Where did Mary lay him. . .

7. Laid him in a manger. . .

Hanukah

Hebrew Folk Song

Ha - nu - kah,   Ha - nu - kah,   mer - ry hol - i - day!

Ha - nu - kah,   Ha - nu - kah,   Time to dance and   play.

Ha - nu - kah,   Ha - nu - kah,   bright the can - dles burn,

Round and round,   round and round, Watch the drey - dl   turn!

Little Candle Fires

Music by S. E. Goldfarb
Words by S. S. Grossman

1. On this night, let us light one lit-tle can-dle fire, —
2. On this night, let us light two lit-tle can-dle fires, —

'Tis a sight, oh, so bright! One lit-tle can-dle fire.——
'Tis a sight, oh, so bright! Two lit-tle can-dle fires.——

More verses may be added by using other numbers (three. . .eight).

Do Your Ears Hang Low?

Traditional

Do your ears hang low? Do they wob-ble to and fro?

Can you tie 'em in a knot? Can you tie 'em in a bow?

Can you toss 'em o-ver your shoul-der like a Con-ti-nen-tal sol-dier?

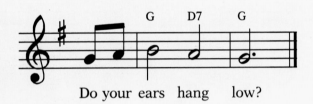

Do your ears hang low?

Dr. Knickerbocker

Playground Game

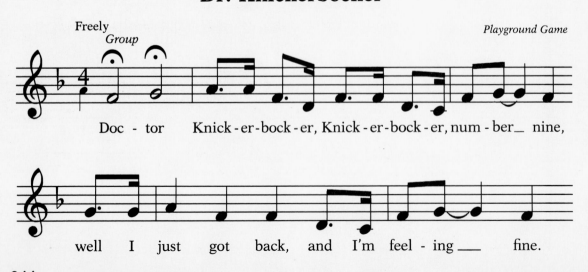

Doc-tor Knick-er-bock-er, Knick-er-bock-er, num-ber___ nine,

well I just got back, and I'm feel-ing___ fine.

Leader   1. Now,   let's get ___ the rhy - thm of   the hands *(clap   clap)*.
Group   Now,   we   got ___ the rhy - thm of   the hands *(clap   clap)*.

Leader   2. Now,   let's get ___ the rhy - thm of   the feet *(stamp stamp)*.
Group   Now,   we   got ___ the rhy - thm of   the feet *(stamp stamp)*.

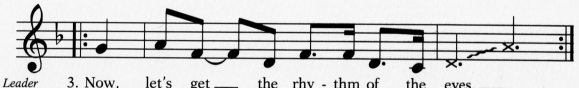

Leader   3. Now,   let's get ___ the rhy - thm of   the eyes. ___
Group   Now,   we   got ___ the rhy - thm of   the eyes. ___

Leader   4. Now,   let's get ___ the rhy - thm of   the hips, whoo - wee!
Group   Now,   we   got ___ the rhy - thm of   the hips, whoo - wee!

Leader

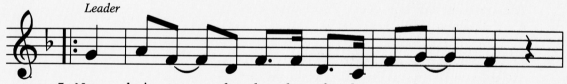

5. Now,   let's get ___ the rhy - thm of   the num - ber ___ nine!

All

One, two, three, four,   five,   six,   sev - en, eight,   nine! _____

The Bus

Play Song

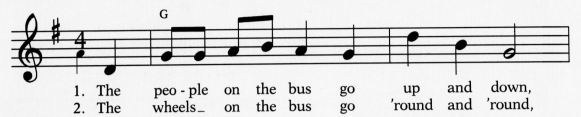

1. The peo-ple on the bus go up and down,
2. The wheels_ on the bus go 'round and 'round,

up and down, up and down. The peo-ple on the bus go
'round and 'round, 'round and 'round. The wheels_ on the bus go

up and down All through the town.
'round and 'round All through the town.

3. The horn on the bus goes "Toot! toot! toot!
Toot! toot! toot! Toot! toot! toot!"
The horn on the bus goes "Toot! toot! toot!"
All through the town.

4. The wiper on the bus goes "Swish! swish! swish!
Swish! swish! swish! Swish! swish! swish!"
The wiper on the bus goes "Swish! swish! swish!"
All through the town.

5. The driver on the bus says "Let them on!
Let them on! Let them on!"
The driver on the bus says, "Let them on!"
All through the town.

I've a Pair of Fishes

Jewish Folk Tune
Words by Lilian Vandevere

1. I've a pair of fish - es, fish - es. They are wash-ing dish - es, dish - es.
2. I've a pair of pup-pies, pup-pies. They are rais - ing gup-pies, gup-pies.

(No repeat first time)

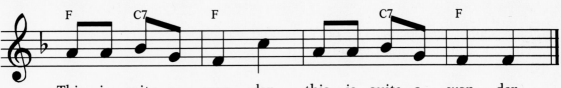

This is in - deed a won - der. See the fish - es wash-ing dish - es.
This is in - deed a won - der. See the pup-pies rais - ing gup-pies.

This is quite a won - der, this is quite a won - der.
This is quite a won - der, this is quite a won - der.

3. I've a pair of foxes, foxes.
   They are building boxes, boxes.
   This is indeed a wonder.
   See the foxes building boxes.
   See the puppies raising guppies.
   See the fishes washing dishes.
   This is quite a wonder,
   This is quite a wonder.

4. I've a pair of bunnies. . .
   They are reading funnies. . .
   See the bunnies reading funnies.
   See the foxes. . .
   See the puppies. . .
   See the fishes. . .

5. I've a pair of parrots. . .
   They are eating carrots. . .
   See the parrots eating carrots.
   See the bunnies. . .
   See the foxes. . .
   See the puppies. . .
   See the fishes. . .

Lucy

Traditional

1. Lu - cy had a ba - by. She named him Ti - ny Tim.
2. He drank up all the wa - ter. He ate up all the soap.

She put him in the bath - tub, To __ teach him how to swim.
He tried to eat the bath - tub, But it wouldn't go down his throat.

3. Lucy called the doctor. The doctor called the nurse.
 The nurse then called the lady with the alligator purse.

Dumplin's

*Calypso Song from the
West Indies*

"Cook - ie ____ are you sure no - bo - dy passed here?" "No, my friend."

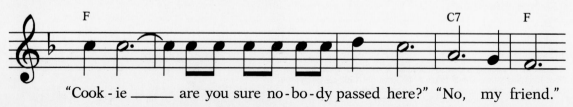

"Cook - ie ____ are you sure no - bo - dy passed here?" "No, my friend."

"Well, {one / two} of my dump-lin's gone." "Don't tell __ me so!"

{"One / "Two} of my dump-lin's gone." "Don't tell me so!" {"One / "Two} of my dump-lin's gone."

The Little Shoemaker

Traditional

There's a lit-tle wee man in a lit-tle wee house, Lives

o-ver the way you see, And he sits at the win-dow and sews all day,

Mak-ing shoes for you and me.

A - rap a-tap tap, A - rap a-tap tap, Hear the ham-mers tit-tat-tee.

A - rap a-tap tap, A - rap a-tap tap, Mak-ing shoes for you and me.

This Old Man

English folk song

1. This old man, he played one, He played nick-nack on my drum.
2. This old man, he played two, He played nick-nack on my shoe.

With a

nick-nack, pad-dy whack, give a dog a bone, This old man came roll-ing home.

3. This old man, he played three,
   He played nick-nack on my tree.

4. This old man, he played four,
   He played nick-nack on my door.

5. This old man, he played five,
   He played nick-nack on my hive.

6. This old man, he played six,
   He played nick-nack on my sticks.

7. This old man, he played seven,
   He played nick-nack on my oven.

8. This old man, he played eight,
   He played nick-nack on my gate.

9. This old man, he played nine,
   He played nick-nack on my line.

10. This old man, he played ten,
    He played nick-nack on my hen.

Oh, My Aunt Came Back

Traditional

1. Oh, my aunt came back, (Oh, my aunt came back,) from Hon - o - lu, (from Hon - o - lu,) And she brought with her (And she brought with her) a wood - en shoe. (a wood - en shoe.)

2. . . . from old Japan. . . a waving fan.

3. . . . from old Algiers. . . a pair of shears.

4. . . . from Guadalupe. . . a Hula-Hoop.

5. . . . from the New York fair. . . a rocking chair.

6. . . . from the City Zoo. . . a monkey like you!

Ten in a Bed

Traditional

1. There were ten in a bed and the lit-tle one said, "Roll o - ver!
2. There were nine in a bed and the lit-tle one said, "Roll o - ver!

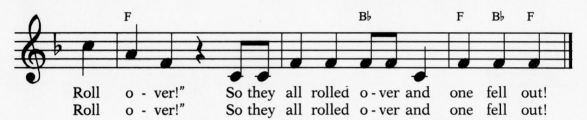

Roll o - ver!" So they all rolled o - ver and one fell out!
Roll o - ver!" So they all rolled o - ver and one fell out!

Verses 3-9:
There were. . . (8, 7, 6, and so on)

Verse 10: There was one in a bed
And the little one said,
(spoken) "Good night!"

Atakata Nuva

Eskimo Hunting Song

At - a - kat - a nu - va, At - a - kat - a nu - va,

Ah mis - a - day, mis - a - do - mis - a - day.

Hex - a col - a - mis - a wa - ta,

Go back to beginning and sing to the End
(Da Capo al Fine)

Hex - a col - a - mis - a wa - ta.

And They Danced

Words and music
by Clara E. Spelman

A fid-dler picked up his bow one day, And he fid-dled a - way.

He fid-dled a - way, And he fid-dled and he fid-dled a - way.

1. A duck heard him play so the duck be - gan to say,
2. A mouse heard him play so the mouse be - gan to say,

(a) "Quack, quack, quack. Quack, quack, quack."
(b) "Squeak-y, squeak-y, squeak. Squeak-y squeak-y squeak."
(to a)

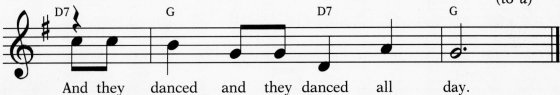

And they danced and they danced all day.

3. A frog heard him play so the frog began to say,
   "Croak, croak, croak. Croak, croak, croak.
   Squeaky. . . Quack. . ." And they danced. . .

4. A cricket heard him play so the cricket began to say,
   "Ticka, ticka, tick. Ticka, ticka, tick.
   Croak. . . Squeaky. . . Quack. . ." And they danced. . .

5. A bee heard him play so the bee began to say,
   "Buzz, buzz, buzz. Buzz, buzz, buzz.
   Ticka. . . Croak. . . Squeaky. . . Quack. . ." And they danced. . .

(Sing *quack* low, *squeaky* high, *croak* low, *ticka* high, and *buzz* low.)

Little Spotted Puppy

Words and music by Lynn Freeman Olson

1. When a lit-tle spot-ted pup-py, Just as nois-y as could be,
2. Oh, it real-ly made me hap-py When I heard that he could stay!

Came to vis-it us in our house, I could tell that he liked me.
Now I help with all his groom-ing, And I feed him ev-'ry day.

'Cause he wig-gled his ears, and he wag-gled his tail,
So, he wig-gles his ears, and he wag-gles his tail,

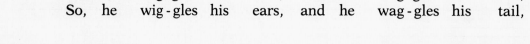

And he barked, and he barked! 'Cause he wig-gled his ears,
and he barks, and he barks! So, he wig-gles his ears,

and he wag-gled his tail, And he barked, and he barked!
and he wag-gles his tail, And he barks, and he barks!

254

Little White Duck

Music by Bernard Zaritsky
Words by Walt Barrows

1. There's a lit-tle white duck, sit-tin' in the wat-er,
2. There's a lit-tle green frog, swim-min' in the wat-er,
3. There's a lit-tle black bug, float-in' in the wat-er,

Lit-tle white duck, do-in' what she ought-er.
Lit-tle green frog, do-in' what he ought-er.
Lit-tle black bug, do-in' what she ought-er.

She took a bite of a lil-y pad,
He jumped right off of the lil-y pad That the
She tickled the frog on the lil-y pad, That the

Flapped her wings and she said, "I'm glad
little duck bit and he said, "I'm glad
little duck bit and she said, "I'm glad

I'm a lit-tle white duck, sit-tin' in the wat-er, Quack, quack, quack."
I'm a lit-tle green frog, swim-min' in the wat-er, Glumph, glumph, glumph."
I'm a lit-tle black bug, float-in' in the wat-er, Chir, chir, chir."

4. There's a little red snake, flyin' in
   the water,
Little red snake, doin' what he oughter.
He frightened the duck and the
   frog so bad,
Ate the little bug and he said,
"I'm glad I'm a little red snake,
flyin' in the water, Hiss, hiss, hiss."

5. Now there's nobody left, sittin' in
   the water,
Nobody left, doin' what he oughter.
There's nothin' left but the lily pad,
The duck and the frog ran away.
It's sad! Now there's nobody left,
sittin' in the water, Boo, hoo, hoo.

Little Sir Echo

*Words and music by
Laura R. Smith and
J. S. Fearis*

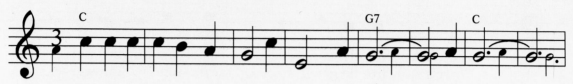

1. Lit-tle Sir Ech-o, how do you do, } Hel-lo, _____ (hel - lo) hel - lo (hel - lo) _____
2. Lit-tle Sir Ech-o, you're ve-ry near,

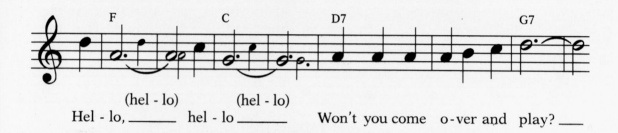

Lit-tle Sir Ech-o, how do you do, } Hel-lo, _____ (hel - lo) hel - lo (hel - lo) _____
Lit-tle Sir Ech-o, you're ve-ry clear,

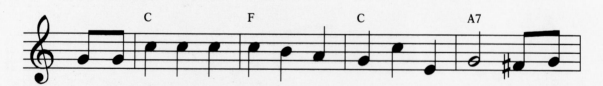

(hel - lo)   (hel - lo)
Hel - lo, _____ hel - lo _____   Won't you come o-ver and play? __

You're a nice lit - tle fel - low, I know by your voice, But you're

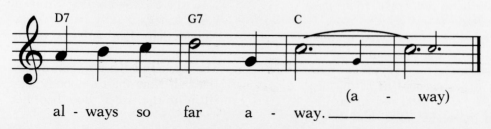

(a - way)
al - ways so far a - way. _____

Obwisana

Song from Ghana

("Oh, I just hurt my finger on a rock.")

Ob - wi - sa - na   sa - na - na   Ob - wi - sa - na   sa.

Ob - wi - sa - na   sa - na - na   Ob - wi - sa - na   sa.

Che Che Koolay

Singing game from Ghana

Che-che koo-lay, che-che koo-lay, Che-che Ko-fee sa che-che Ko-fee sa

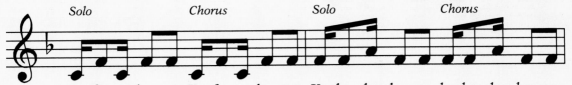

Ko-fee sa-lan-ga, Ko-fee sa-lan-ga. Ka-ka-shee lan-ga, ka-ka-shee lan-ga.

Koom - ma-dye-day, Koom - ma-dye-day.

La Muñeca

Spanish Folk Song

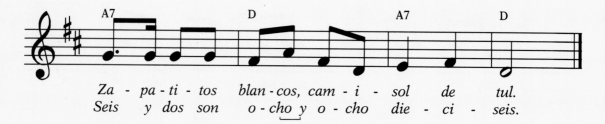

1. Ten-go un-a mu - ñe - ca ves - ti - da de a - zul;
2. Dos y dos son cua-tro, y cua-tro y dos son seis,

Za - pa - ti - tos blan - cos, cam - i - sol de tul.
Seis y dos son o - cho y o - cho die - ci - seis.

Michael, Row the Boat Ashore

Folk Song from the Bahamas

Mi-chael row the boat a - shore, Hal - le - lu - jah!

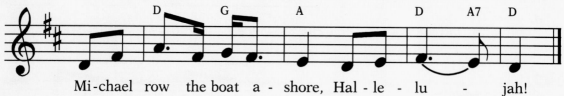

Mi-chael row the boat a - shore, Hal - le - lu - jah!

258

Shake the Papaya Down

Calypso Song
Collected by W. S. Haynie

Ma - ma says no play; This is a work - day.

Up with the bright sun; Get all the work done.

If you will help me, Climb up the tall tree,

Shake the pa - pa - ya down.

Supercalifragilisticexpialidocious

Music by Richard M. Sherman
Words by Robert B. Sherman

1. Sup-er-cal - i - frag-il - is-tic - ex-pi-al - i - do-cious!
2. Sup-er-cal - i - frag-il - is-tic - ex-pi-al - i - do-cious!

E - ven though the sound of it is some-thing quite a - tro-cious,
Sup-er-cal - i - frag-il - is-tic - ex-pi - al - i - do-cious!

If you say it loud e-nough, you'll al-ways sound pre - co-cious.
Sup-er-cal - i - frag-il - is - tic - ex-pi - al - i - do-cious!

Sup-er-cal - i - frag-il - is-tic - ex-pi-al - i - do-cious!
Sup-er-cal - i - frag-il - is-tic - ex-pi-al - i - do-cious!

When the Train Comes Along

American Folk Song

Refrain

When the train comes a-long, _ when the train comes a-long, _

I'll meet you at the sta - tion

End
(Fine)

when the train comes a - long.

Verse

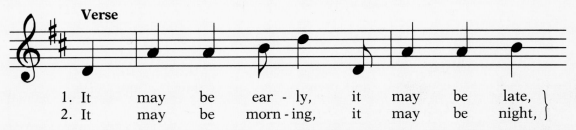

1. It may be ear - ly, it may be late,
2. It may be morn - ing, it may be night,

Go back to the beginning and sing to the End.
(Da Capo al Fine)

But I'll meet you at the sta - tion when the train comes a-long.

The Railroad Train

Charles Harvey

1. Click - et - y clack, a - lunk, a - lunk!
2. O - ver the bridge, a - cross the lake,

A train is com - ing, a - chunk, a - chunk;
A mile a min - ute, it has to make;

A click - et - y clack a mile a - way;
A ter - ri - ble snake, with flam - ing eyes,

It has - n't a sec - ond o' time to stay;
That wig - gles and wig - gles a - long the ties,

It sings a nois - y clack - et - y song,
The cin - ders fall in fi - er - y rain,

A rick - et - y, rock - et - y, rack - et - y song,
A tun - nel is wait - ing to swal - low the train,

"You're on the track, get out of the way go 'long!" ___
Good - bye, good - bye! To - mor - row he'll come a - gain! ___

Tender Shepherd

Music by Mark Charlap
Words by Carolyn Leigh

1. Ten - der shep - herd, ten - der shep - herd
2. Ten - der shep - herd, ten - der shep - herd

watch - es o - ver all his sheep.
you for - got to count your sheep.

One, say your prayers and two, close your eyes and
One, in the mea - dow; two, in the gar - den;

three, safe and hap - pi - ly fall a - sleep.
three, in the nur - ser - y fast a - sleep.

All Night, All Day

Refrain

African American Spiritual

All night, all __ day, An-gels watch-ing o-ver me, my Lord. __

All night, all __ day, An-gels watch-ing o-ver me.

Verse

Now I lay me down _ to sleep, An-gels watch-ing o-ver me, my Lord. __

Pray the Lord my soul _ to keep, An-gels watch-ing o-ver me.

By'm Bye

Folk Song from Texas

1. By'm bye, By'm bye. Stars shin-ing
2. By'm bye, By'm bye. Stars shin-ing

Num-ber, num-ber one, num-ber two,
Num-ber, num-ber six, num-ber sev-en,

num-ber three, num-ber four, num-ber five,
num-ber eight, num-ber nine, num-ber ten,

Oh my!
Oh my! By'm bye, by'm bye,

Oh my! By'm bye, by'm bye.

Bibbidi-Bobbidi-Boo
(The Magic Song)
From Walt Disney's "Cinderella"

Words and Music by Mack David
Al Hoffman
Jerry Livingston

Sa - la-ga-doo-la men-chic-ka-boo-la BIB-BI-DI-BOB-BI-DI-BOO

Put 'em to-ge-ther and what have you got? BIB-BI-DI-BOB-BI-DI-BOO.

Sa - la-ga-doo-la men-chic-ka-boo-la BIB-BI-DI-BOB-BI-DI-BOO.

It-'ll do mag-ic be-lieve it or not,   BIB-BI-DI-BOB-BI-DI-BOO.

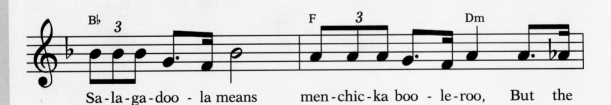

Sa-la-ga-doo - la means   men-chic-ka boo - le-roo,   But the

Thing-a-ma-bob that does the job is BIB-BI-DI-BOB-BI-DI-BOO.

Sa - la - ga - doo - la men - chic - ka - boo - la BIB - BI - DI - BOB - BI - DI - BOO.

Put 'em to - ge - ther and what have you got? BIB - BI - DI - BOB - BI - DI - BOO.

BIB - BI - DI - BOB - BI - DI - BIB - BI - DI - BOB - BI - DI - BIB - BI - DI - BOB - BI - DI - BOO.

"BIBBIDI-BOBBIDI-BOO"
© 1948 Walt Disney Music Company
Words by Jerry Livingston
Music by Mack David and Al Hoffman

Chicken Soup with Rice

Music by Carole King
Words by Maurice Sendak

In January it's so nice while slipping on the sliding ice
to sip hot chicken soup with rice.
Sipping once, sipping twice, sipping chicken soup with rice.

In February it will be my snowman's anniversary
with cake for him and soup for me!
Happy once, happy twice, happy chicken soup with rice.

In March the wind blows down the door and spills my soup upon the floor.
It laps it up and roars for more.
Blowing once, blowing twice, blowing chicken soup with rice.

In April I will go away to far off Spain or old Bombay
and dream about hot soup all day.
Oh my once, oh my twice, oh my, oh chicken soup with rice.

In May I truly think it best to be a robin lightly dressed
concocting soup inside my nest.
Mix it once, mix it twice, mix that chicken soup with rice.

In June I saw a charming group of roses all begin to droop.
I pepped them up with chicken soup!
Sprinkle once, sprinkle twice, sprinkle chicken soup with rice.

In July I'll take a peep into the cool and fishy deep
where chicken soup is selling cheap.
Selling once, selling twice, selling chicken soup with rice.

In August it will be so hot. I will become a cooking pot
cooking soup of course. Why not?
Cooking once, cooking twice, cooking chicken soup with rice.

In September for a while I will ride a crocodile
down the chicken soupy Nile.
Paddle once, paddle twice, paddle chicken soup with rice.

In October I'll be host to witches, goblins and a ghost.
I'll serve them chicken soup on toast.
Whoopy once, whoopy twice, whoopy chicken soup with rice.

In November's gusty gale I will flop my flippy tail
and spout hot soup. I'll be a whale!
Spouting once, spouting twice, spouting chicken soup with rice.

In December I will be a baubled, bangled Christmas tree
with soup bowls draped all over me.
Merry once, merry twice, merry chicken soup with,
merry chicken soup with, merry chicken soup with rice.

I told you once, I told you twice, all seasons of the year are nice
for eating chicken soup, eating chicken soup with rice!
(Chicken soup, chicken soup with rice.)

I Live in a City

Words and music by
Malvina Reynolds

Refrain

I live in a cit-y, yes, I do, I live in a cit-y,

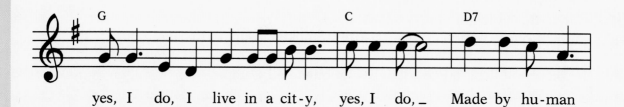

yes, I do, I live in a cit-y, yes, I do, _ Made by hu-man

End (Fine) **Verse**

hands.

1. Black hands, white hands, yel-low and brown,
2. Brown hands, yel-low hands, white _ and black,

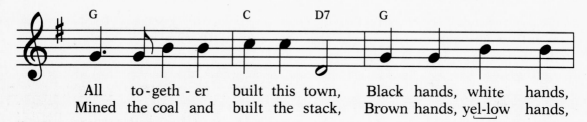

All to-geth-er built this town, Black hands, white hands,
Mined the coal and built the stack, Brown hands, yel-low hands,

Go back to the beginning and sing to End.
(Da Capo al Fine)

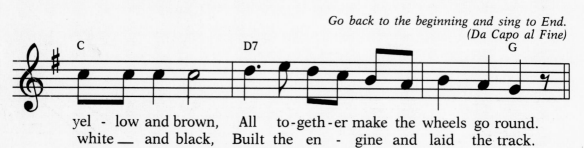

yel - low and brown, All to-geth-er make the wheels go round.
white _ and black, Built the en - gine and laid the track.

3. Black hands, brown hands, yellow and white,
   Built the buildings tall and bright,
   Black hands, brown hands, yellow and white,
   Filled them all with shining light.

4. Black hands, white hands, brown and tan,
   Milled the flour and cleaned the pan,
   Black hands, white hands, brown and tan,
   The working woman and the working man.

Sing Me a Song

*Words and music
by Barbara Staton*

1. Sing me a song, not ve - ry long.
2. Sing me a *so.* Sing me a *mi.*

Sing all to - geth - er, sing out strong.
Sing me a *do mi la mi so.*

When things go wrong, Sing, sing a song.
Sing me a *so.* Sing me a *mi.*

Hoo - ray! You're o - kay, Just sing a hap - py song.
Hoo - *re* sing a *so la* down to *mi re do.*

GLOSSARY OF TERMS

accent (>) a single sound louder than those around it, **126**

bar line a line that divides notes on a staff into sets, **109**

beat the basic unit of time in music, **2**

brass family instruments including French horn, trombone, trumpet, and tuba, **140**

canon a musical form in which the same melody is sung by two or more voices beginning at different times so they overlap, **38**

coda a short ending section, **113**

contrast a thing that is very different from something else, **193**

crescendo (————) to get louder gradually, **54**

decrescendo (————) to get softer gradually, **55**

dotted half note (𝅗𝅥.), **122**

dotted quarter note (♩.), **154**

eighth note (♪), **29, 154**

form the order of sections in music, **40**

forte loud, **200**

half note (𝅗𝅥), **86**

melody the tune of a series of pitches moving upward, downward, or staying the same, **169**

note a symbol for how long a musical sound lasts, **5**

pattern the order of pitches or rhythms, **7**

percussion family instruments that are struck, shaken, or scraped to produce a sound, **141**

phrase a short section of music that is one musical thought, **118**

piano soft, **200**

pitch the highness or lowness of a sound, **5**

quarter note (♩), **29**

quarter rest (𝄽), **29**

repeat signs (𝄆   𝄇), **79**

rest a sign for silence in music, **16**

rhyme sounds at the end of lines of verse that sound alike, **68**

rhythm long sounds, short sounds, or long and short sounds heard one after the other, **9**

rhythm pattern an organized group of long and short sounds heard again and again, **57**

rondo a musical form in which the first section is repeated several times with a different section between each of the repeats, **169**

section a part of the whole, **40**

staff the lines and spaces on which music is written, **5**

string family instruments such as violin, harp, and cello that are sounded by plucking, or drawing a bow across strings, **138**

strong beat the first beat after each bar line, **65**

texture the thickness or thinness of sound that results when tones are played or sung together, **204**

tone color the sound that is special to each voice or instrument, **210**

verse words and music that make up the body of a song and that may alternate with the refrain, **15**

woodwind family instruments including bassoon, oboe, clarinet, and flute, **139**

CLASSIFIED INDEX

274

LISTENING SELECTIONS

ALPHABETICAL SONG INDEX